POSTERS OF THE FIRST WORLD WAR

David Bownes & Robert Fleming

 SHIRE

NATIONAL
ARMY
MUSEUM

Published in Great Britain in 2014 by Shire Publications Ltd, PO Box 883, Oxford, OX1 9PL, UK.
PO Box 3985, New York, NY 10185–3985, USA.
E-mail: shire@shirebooks.co.uk   www.shirebooks.co.uk

Shire General no. 8.   ISBN-13: 978 0 74781 428 3

Printed in China through Worldprint Ltd.

14 15 16 17 18   10 9 8 7 6 5 4 3 2 1

ACKNOWLEDGEMENTS

Images are acknowledged as follows: Alamy page 22; Galerie Bilderwelt / The Bridgeman Art Library pages 24, 31 and 127; The Imperial War Museum pages 45 (PST 12424), 95 (PST 13632), 123 (PST 13657), 125 (PST 12226), 129 (PST 12216), 131 (PST 12208), 133 (PST 12586), 135 (PST 12426), 141 (PST5471), 145 (PST 13369), 147 (PST 12243), 155 (PST 13169), 158 & 161 (PST 10424) and 163 (PST10424); Library of Congress, page 91 (German poster) and page 151; London Transport Museum pages 13 and 75; Science and Society Picture Library page 5.
All remaining posters are from the National Army Museum's collections.

NOTE ON CAPTIONING

Wherever possible the names and dates of known artists have been included in the caption, together with details of the publisher.

CONTENTS

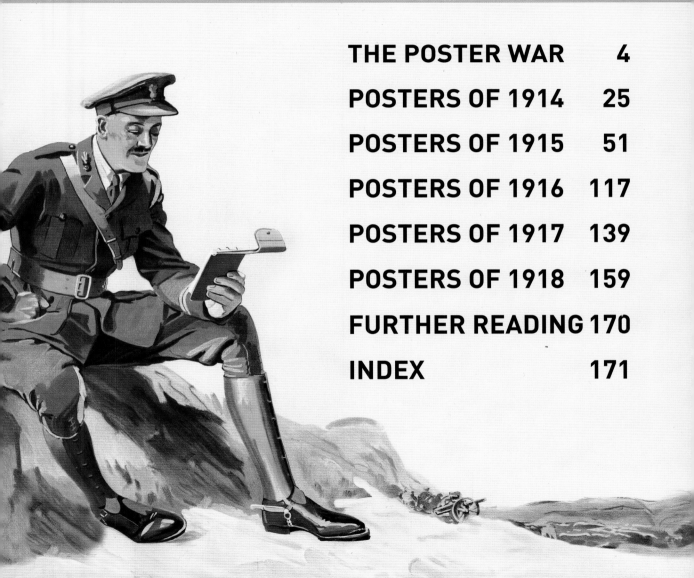

THE POSTER WAR

The Great War (1914–18) was the first truly modern conflict, fought on a global and industrial scale. It required the complete mobilisation of the countries involved, resulting in unparalleled state intervention into the lives of ordinary people, from conscription to the employment of women, food rationing and the gradual imposition of restrictions affecting many aspects of daily life. Communicating these changes effectively, while maintaining public morale, was recognised by all warring nations as an essential element in securing military victory. In an age before the Internet, television or radio, posters emerged as the ideal medium for mass communication, seized upon by governments, private organisations, charities and even retailers to get their war messages across to the widest possible audience. In this respect, posters were especially suited to the task at hand as they could be cheaply produced in very large numbers and distributed in a range of sizes to maximise potential display opportunities.

At the outset of the war in August 1914, the poster was already a mature advertising tool, which had developed over centuries from crude letterpress notices to sophisticated full-colour lithographs. Continental posters, in particular, had established a reputation for considerable artistic merit, pioneered by the likes of Jules Chéret, Henri de Toulouse-Lautrec and Alphonse Mucha during the late nineteenth century. In Britain commercial artists, including Dudley Hardy and the 'poster king', John Hassall, popularised a distinctive domestic approach, typified by the use of bold flat colour, a central (often comic) figure and a short direct slogan (see *Skegness is SO*

John Hassall's famous railway poster promoting the bracing qualities of Skegness (1908). The vivid use of colour and a short emphasised message ('SO Bracing') was to prove influential on the design of wartime recruiting posters.

V. R.

HER MAJESTY THE QUEEN

having deemed it desirable to commemorate the bravery shown by the Irish Regiments in the recent operations in South Africa, has been graciously pleased to command that an Irish Regiment of Foot Guards be formed.

THE REGIMENT WILL BE CALLED THE

"IRISH GUARDS."

The Age and Standard of Recruits are as for other Regiments of Foot Guards, viz.:—

AGE: 18 TO 25 YEARS.

MINIMUM HEIGHT: **5** feet **7** inches for men under **20** years of age.

5 feet **8** inches for men **20** years of age and over.

Chest Measurement varies with the height.

MEN OF GOOD CHARACTER ARE INVITED TO JOIN.

They should apply to_____ or to any Recruiter, from whom the conditions of service and all particulars can be obtained.

Recruits on enlistment will be sent to join the Guards Depot at Caterham, Surrey.

A Guards' Employment Society has been established for the purpose of assisting Soldiers of the Foot Guards in obtaining work in Civil Life on their transfer to the Reserve or on discharge.

General Advantages of the Army.

A pamphlet showing the conditions of service in the Army and containing full information as regards Food, Clothing, Quarters, Fuel and Light, Medical Attendance, Prizes for Good Shooting, Libraries, Recreation Rooms, Army Schools, &c., &c., will be supplied free on application at any Post Office, or from any Recruiter.

GOD SAVE THE QUEEN.

PRINTED FOR HER MAJESTY'S STATIONERY OFFICE BY HAZELL, WATSON & VINEY, LD., 52, LONG ACRE, LONDON, W.C.

Bracing). Together with the fledgling advertising industry, and supported by the patronage of leading retailers, manufacturers, theatres and transport companies, such artists helped to create a visual language for the poster which dominated the hoardings in the years before the war and was well understood by consumers.

The pre-war display of posters in Europe and the United States was subject to varying degrees of regulation, although advertising was regarded as a defining, and often unwelcome, characteristic of most urban environments. Posters could be seen everywhere: in the streets, at the railway station, on the sides of buses and trams, in shop windows – almost anywhere, in fact, where people congregated. Government notices, however, were usually easy to distinguish from the mass of pictorial commercial posters that jostled for the attention of the passer-by. Official proclamations and injunctions were often printed in text-only format, headed by the royal arms or some other symbol of the state.

This was to change during the war, as governments across Europe appropriated the design values, and display space, of commercial advertising. New venues were found for 'war posters' in banks, schools, churches, libraries, factories, offices and rural settings. At first, the sheer number of war-related posters threatened to swamp available sites, a situation eventually eased by the introduction of printing restrictions caused by paper shortages. As an indication of the scale of production, the British Museum renounced its pre-war right to a copy of every poster printed in the United Kingdom for reference purposes. Luckily other institutions, most notably the Imperial War Museum in London, set about collecting representative samples from the combatant nations, resulting in the survival of thousands of individual designs.

A typical pre-First World War British Army recruiting poster, in this case announcing the formation of the Irish Guards (1900) for service in the Boer War. Information about the terms and conditions of service is printed below the royal monogram of Queen Victoria, indicating that this is an official government notice.

Taken as a whole, these surviving posters provide a remarkable visual history of the war, with similar themes recurring on both sides of the conflict, underlining the need for all governments to secure the consent of their citizens through persuasion and propaganda. Posters, of course, were not the only method of communication available, and should be viewed alongside the wide variety of official and non-official channels of information, including newspapers, publications, films, plays, songs, cartoons and public meetings. Neither were all, or indeed most, wartime posters produced by government agencies alone. In fact, it is striking how many of the surviving posters were independently printed by private organisations in support of the war effort or on behalf of specific charities, thereby helping to foster a sense of shared endeavour between the government and the people.

The creation of a sense of shared endeavour, however, often masked deep-seated national tensions. In Britain, for example, the years immediately before the war had been marked by industrial unrest, an Irish crisis, suffragette militancy and constitutional difficulties, to say nothing of the growing independent spirit of the British Empire's dominions. Against this background, posters were a useful tool to achieve social unity, while open dissent about the war was effectively censored under the terms of the Defence of the Realm Act (1914).

The posters featured in this publication have been primarily selected from the archives of the National Army Museum, London, with a corresponding focus on the experience of Britain and its empire during the war. Many of the themes discussed, such as the recruitment drive of 1914–15 and government war loans, have close parallels with the wartime poster campaigns of other nations. But there were notable differences in the United Kingdom, including the delayed introduction of conscription, a more hands-off approach by government and the existence of a highly developed advertising industry (second only to the United States), which created a uniquely British response. So, too, did Britain's relationship with her imperial subjects, especially in the economically advanced dominions of Australia, New Zealand, South Africa and Canada, where posters proved to be an important tool in tapping the vast pool of potential volunteer recruits.

The types of posters produced in Britain during the war can be broken down into four broad categories: recruitment (including justifying the war), government fund-raising, the Home Front and 'business as usual'. The last includes the great mass of commercial advertising that continued to be printed throughout the war, almost in defiance of the conflict taking place across the Channel. Wartime photographs of street scenes are striking in their inclusion of posters promoting pre-war domestic products and entertainments, often sitting uneasily next to calls for young men to enlist or requests for conscientious citizens to 'eat less bread' in support of the war effort. Some manufacturers, such as Oxo and Dunlop Tyres, featured soldiers in their advertising as a patriotic gesture, while others switched their focus to manufacturing wartime necessities (see *The Studington Military Kit*, 1915). Such posters may have helped to unite the Home Front with the war theatres, but they also blurred the division between official (i.e. government-endorsed) and unofficial notices. As the war progressed, this blurring of origin became more pronounced, but it was largely inevitable as both types of poster were often produced by the same designers working for the same advertising agencies.

The reason for this lies in the government's reliance on the advertising industry to provide images for official poster campaigns. Until 1918, there was no centralised Ministry of Information to offer strategic leadership in the direction of such campaigns. Instead, posters were issued at different stages in the war by a range of government agencies, including the Parliamentary Recruiting Committee (PRC), the Parliamentary (later National) War Savings

Committee, the Ministry of National Service and the Ministry of Food. A War Propaganda Bureau (known as Wellington House) had been established in 1914 under the leadership of Charles Masterman, but its focus was on influencing opinion overseas, especially in the neutral United States, through the publication of books, pamphlets, periodicals, films, photographs, lantern slides and postcards. Meanwhile, the task of recruiting a volunteer army to rival the conscripted forces of continental Europe fell to the recently formed PRC – a body of bureaucrats, clerks and administrators lacking in-house marketing expertise. Some guidance was provided by the former soldier and advertising professional Hedley Le Bas, who as proprietor of the Caxton Agency, had been tasked by the government to 'advertise for an army' before the war and was to remain an influential figure throughout the conflict. Under his influence, the PRC established an Advisory Committee to review standards of poster design, but more often than not the PRC was content to accept speculative submissions from commercial printers, or even to re-use existing advertising to get its message across (see *The Veteran's Farewell*, 1914). In total, the PRC employed at least thirty-six different poster printers, with one firm, David Allen & Sons, providing 25 per cent of the designs. The result was a mixed bag of images and messages, occasionally reaching very high standards (especially when the PRC made a rare foray into direct commissioning), but more often resulting in mediocre posters drawn by anonymous artists.

The first recruiting posters published by the government followed a traditional text-based format, some of which gave detailed instructions on how and where to join up. The response was initially overwhelming, with almost half a million men volunteering by mid-September 1914. But afterwards the numbers of new recruits fell steadily, resulting in the issue of more dramatic, pictorial designs by the PRC that, whatever their individual merit, added a fresh dynamism to the recruiting campaign. Often designed by advertisers, these new posters addressed the ordinary man as a free-thinking individual, basing his decision to enlist on a variety of persuasive factors. Chief amongst these was the depiction of Germany as the aggressor who had illegally invaded Belgium, despite the existence of international treaties protecting Belgian neutrality. Civilians were asked to 'remember Belgium' when making their decision, in the same way that later posters used the sinking of the *Lusitania* (1915) and the bombing of London (1915–18) as justifications for the prosecution of the war. In a clever marketing ploy, which shows the influence of commercial thinking, onlookers were encouraged to see themselves in the poster images. For this reason, serving soldiers were invariably depicted as ordinary privates or sergeants (never officers) cheerfully calling on their civilian equivalents to join them in a common cause and embark on a patriotic adventure.

The government's efforts were joined by local recruiting agencies (such as the London Recruiting Depot), private companies and newspapers, which demonstrated their patriotism by publishing their own recruiting posters. The best of these were often of greater artistic merit and power than those accepted by the PRC, including Alfred Leete's famous drawing of Lord Kitchener for *London Opinion* (1914) and the designs commissioned by London Underground from Gerald Spencer Pryse, among others.

When it became clear that the war would not be over by Christmas 1914, as many had optimistically hoped, the message of recruiting posters gradually changed. More emphasis was placed on duty, especially to King and Country, but there were also direct appeals to groups of neighbours, co-workers, sportsmen and graduates to form 'Pals' Battalions', where friends could serve together (see *Hurry up! Boys*, 1915).

The decline in recruitment continued, however, as 1915 wore on. This in turn led the PRC to publish a notorious group of posters that sought to shame young men into joining up by implying that they were 'shirkers' avoiding their patriotic responsibilities. The best known of these, including *Daddy, what did YOU Do In the Great War?* and *GO! It's Your Duty Lad,* were both emotionally powerful and unpopular. But they were atypical of the PRC's output and, like the majority of the 164 designs the Committee published between 1914 and 1915, had been speculatively submitted by commercial printers rather than commissioned as part of a directed campaign.

Following the introduction of conscription to Great Britain in 1916, the PRC's efforts were redirected to support the sale of government bonds organised by the National War Savings Committee. In other parts of the British Empire recruitment remained voluntary, resulting in a range of regional recruiting campaigns and posters. Normally directed by government agencies, such as the New South Wales Recruiting Committee or the Department of Recruiting for Ireland, the majority of these posters stressed historic links with Britain as the 'mother country', even when that relationship had been strained by recent unrest and even war. They also played on notions of ethnic 'Britishness', especially in Canada, where posters addressed 'Irish' and 'Scottish' Canadians. In Australia, a number of posters stressed perceived notions of Australian manliness, illustrated through sporting prowess and a commitment to stand by your 'mates' in times of trouble.

Back in the United Kingdom, the drive to sell government War Bonds and Loans resulted in a massive publicity campaign, including over two hundred designs. As with the earlier recruiting posters, notices were printed in a variety of sizes, ranging from the 'double

A massive War Bonds poster dominates the façade of London's Royal Exchange in about 1917. Interestingly, much of the commercial advertising on the bus sides is for non-war-related products and entertainment, showing how the two forms of 'advertising' co-existed.

crown' format (30 inches by 20 inches) favoured by advertisers, to massive one-off versions for fund-raising events, such as the War Bonds poster that dominated the façade of the Royal Exchange in 1917 (see photograph on page 13). On the whole, the quality of these designs was somewhat better than the recruiting posters of 1914–15, possibly because the advertisers who submitted them (again, few were directly commissioned) were more comfortable selling a distinct product, rather than concepts such as patriotism and duty. The fund-raising posters also inspired some excellent designs from well-known artists and illustrators, including Frank Brangwyn and Bert Thomas. The familiar tropes of the recruiting campaign, however, were never far from the surface. Buying a War Bond was invariably presented as a patriotic act, while the earlier injunction to *Enlist Now!* was replaced with the equally strident *Invest Now!*

Independently of government direction, charitable organisations produced probably the most varied and numerous types of 'war poster'. In addition to established bodies such as the Red Cross and the YMCA, over ten thousand new charities sprang up during the First World War to provide assistance for refugees, wounded servicemen, the families of soldiers killed in action, and many other war-related causes. Fund-raising events, meetings and calls for volunteers were all publicised by posters, with the larger organisations (such as the National Committee for the Relief of Belgium) producing dozens of individual designs. The work of these charities lent tacit support to the government's war aims, while the posters they produced reinforced notions of patriotism and personal duty.

Also aimed at the Home Front were government posters intended to modify behaviour in the interest of conserving resources. Produced by a range of government agencies, posters and associated publicity campaigns encouraged salvage, thrift and the avoidance of waste (especially food). For the first time, the public was advised on what it should eat and instructed to make personal sacrifices in support of the wider war effort, including using less fuel and recycling clothing rather than buying new.

Perhaps the most striking change for traditionalists imbued with firm views on domestic roles was the reappraisal of 'women's work' and its place in securing victory. At the start of the war, recruiting posters typically depicted women as dependent on male protection or as old-fashioned mothers. From 1916, posters called on young women to replace men in the munitions factories, in transport jobs and on the land. The formation of the Women's Army Auxiliary Corps (December 1916), and its equivalents in the Navy (1917) and Air Force (1918), also offered women the opportunity to serve in direct support of the armed forces – a situation which would have been unthinkable just a few years before.

So how successful were these posters in getting their message across? Viewed in hindsight, many of the designs appear over-optimistic and even misleading. The more cheery images, in particular, hardly seem serious enough to convey the enormity of world war with its attendant horrors of destruction and death – an aspect of the conflict that is almost always absent. Yet this is, of course, to see the posters from a modern perspective, mediated by a century of reinterpretation and a suspicion of 'propaganda' that developed only slowly during the war itself. Adults viewing 'war posters' in 1914 had been born in the Victorian era and schooled in a very different way of looking at the world and their personal obligations to society. This is not to say that everyone embraced the onset of war, or accepted at face value the messages of the hoardings, but it does remind us that the contemporary

OVERLEAF: A group of new recruits outside an unidentified recruiting office in about November 1914. Among the posters on display are two published by the Parliamentary Recruiting Committee (*Men of the Empire To Arms!* and *Fall In*) together with a poster produced by Associated Newspapers (*Will They Never Come?*), showing that official and unofficial posters were often displayed together.

OFFER YOUR SERVICES NOW.
RECRUITING
OFFICE
10 to 1
2 to 5
6 to 8
6 to 8
"FALL IN"
Will they never come?

audience for war posters interpreted them with a mindset and a partial understanding of the unfolding conflict that is impossible to recreate today. Against this background, posters that positively reinforced existing beliefs and attitudes, such as patriotism and duty, found a more receptive market than similar images would now.

It remains, however, very difficult to assess the effect of posters alone on influencing mass behaviour. Posters were invariably part of larger publicity campaigns and subject to myriad external factors that impacted on their success. The introduction of conscription in 1916, for example, does not necessarily imply that the earlier British recruiting posters had been a failure, only that the government was no longer able to sustain voluntary enlistment. It is possible, though, to draw some broad conclusions regarding the public's reaction to war posters, which hint at their overall effectiveness.

Throughout the war government posters were frequently, and positively, reviewed in the press. Contemporary accounts and photographs also illustrate that they were an everyday part of life, as a correspondent for the *Manchester Guardian* pointed out (not entirely favourably) in April 1915:

> *It is impossible to escape the war posters. They grip you everywhere. They assault you from every corner. They take you in the street and in the trains. They threaten, persuade, cajole and frighten. Every taxi-cab cries out at you in forty different [musical] sharps and flats, and the only way out of the noise is to get inside. You look on one hand and you see, 'If this cap fits you, join at once'. You look on the other, and you are asked what the girls and the grandchildren will think of you if you hold back. Ahead of you Lord Kitchener bars the way with a terrible look and menacing finger, 'I want you'. The eye is subjected to a 'blockade' where everything is contraband but recruiting appeals.*

More typical pieces praised the message and artistry of new issues, while many readers felt moved to write letters testifying to the posters' effectiveness in securing new recruits in their areas and asking how they might obtain additional copies. Few, though, went quite as far as W. H. Hudsmith, who penned some truly awful doggerel for the *Dover Express and East Kent News* (24 September 1915), which nevertheless demonstrates how ubiquitous the war poster had become:

The Posters on the Wall

They've sung the song 'Your King and Country need you'
Said 'Join your Army chums and happy be!'
The girls when you return, they've also told you,
Will tribute osculatory give thee

And those whose biz it is to do recruiting,
Have done right well, and made no end of fuss;
There's tempting bait in every street, on hoarding,
Pictures of bursting shrapnel on the bus.

There's one which shows the pretty little homestead,
'Is this lot not worth fighting for,' they say;
And who untouched looks on the grey haired mother,
Heedless of self, she bravely points the way.

There's the charming one, and dear old Jack, a-trailing,
The Red, White, Blue, its colours never fade,
But the latest one that comes our eyes assailing,
It surely puts all others in the shade.

Once in a while, Divine and inspiration
Cometh to Statesman, Artist, Poet, Seer,

Thanks, thanks to him who found that Army ration
Will give an added flavour to your beer.

Of course, the press operated under wartime reporting restrictions and was expected to support the war effort. Serving soldiers, on the other hand, tended to take a more ironic view of the posters that had encouraged them to join up. According to the historian Nicholas Hiley, by 1917 the slogan *Daddy, what did YOU Do In the Great War?* was being used by front-line troops to express the black humour of their predicament. There is evidence, too, that the government's more commercially inspired poster designs (typified by an often bullying tone) met with a mixed response on the Home Front, a point discussed in more detail in the image captions of this book. Indeed, from the outset of the war there were reports of posters being torn down in protest at their message or criticised by those opposed to the war. James Houston, a Glasgow schoolteacher, for example, was charged in October 1915 with making 'statements likely to prejudice recruiting' when he publicly denounced a recruiting poster for depicting a mother instructing her son to enlist.

Government fund-raising and Home Front posters tended to meet with less criticism, although not everyone appreciated the interference of the state in their daily lives. The campaigns to sell War Loans and Bonds were especially successful, suggesting that the very wide distribution of posters in support of these aims chimed with the public mood and played an important role in helping to raise money to pursue the war to its ultimate conclusion. Exhibitions of war posters (such as one held at the Mansard Gallery of Heals department store in 1917), and their reproduction in colour magazines and as cigarette cards, also testify to the popular appeal of many designs during the conflict itself.

After 1918, the reputation of Britain's wartime posters was irrevocably tarnished by the first-hand accounts of returning veterans, whose bitter experiences implied that conditions at the front had been deliberately obscured by patriotic slogans at home. For some, Great War propaganda (including posters) was now associated with lies and falsehood – a view which has coloured our perception ever since. Art critics and, ironically, the advertising industry lent weight to this view by dismissing domestic wartime posters as vulgar, sentimental and inferior to those produced in Germany and Austria. Writing in 1920, Martin Hardie and Arthur Sabin concluded that 'even about the best of our war posters one feels that they are too often enlarged drawings, excellent as lithographs to preserve in the collector's portfolio, but ineffective when valued in relation to the essential services that a poster is required to render' (*War Posters Issued by Belligerent and Neutral Nations, 1914–19*). Others took an even more negative view. Cyril Sheldon, author of *A History of Poster Advertising* (1937), thought that most British war posters had been 'poor things in point of design, though it may be they served their purpose'. There was some praise for the work of artist-designers, such as Frank Brangwyn and Paul Nash, but more typically reviews of British poster development published in the 1920s and 1930s (of which there were many) drew a veil over the period 1914–18. An unexpected voice in support of Britain's war posters came from Adolf Hitler, who argued in *Mein Kampf* (1925) that 'the British … war propaganda was psychologically correct. By displaying the German to their own people as a barbarian and a Hun, they were preparing the individual soldier for the horrors of war and so helped to spare him disappointments.' This was not, however, a view that would have found much favour in Britain at the time.

More recently, a series of excellent histories has enabled an impartial reappraisal of the importance of posters during the war (see 'Further Reading'). Perhaps one of the greatest tributes to the power of wartime posters is the extent to which they have become part of

STÜTZT UNSRE
FELDGRAUEN

ZEREISST
ENGLANDS
~MACHT~
ZEICHNET

KRIEGSANLEIHE

DRUCK V. WILH. EISFELLER·CÖLN

OTTO LEHMANN·CÖLN

the popular memory of the First World War, with the best-known examples frequently recycled as visual symbols of the war itself. As the images and captions in this book show, the posters themselves often hold complex meanings and nuances not immediately obvious to a modern audience; once deciphered, they reveal a surprising insight into the preoccupations and self-image of Britain during the conflict and the resolve that helped to secure victory in 1918.

In compiling the captions for the posters featured in this volume, the authors would like to acknowledge the help and support of colleagues at the National Army Museum, especially Dr Alastair Massie, Jenny Spencer-Smith, and Ariel Nicole Keeton, and also James Taylor (author of *Your Country Needs You: The Secret History of the Propaganda Poster*) for his advice and comments on the draft. The authors would also like to acknowledge the pioneering research of Dr Nicholas Hiley (Head of the British Cartoon Archive at the Templeman Library, University of Kent), together with the published work of Maurice Rickards, Jim Aulich, John Hewitt and others, which has transformed the study of First World War posters and provided inspiration for this book.

A striking German poster by Otto Lehmann of the type much admired by post-war art critics in Britain. 'Even before the war', wrote Hardie and Sabin in 1920, 'we had much to learn from the concentrated power, the force of design, the economy of means, which made German posters sing out from a wall like a defiant blare of trumpets. Their posters issued during the War are even more aggressive ... [and] have a force and character that make most of our own seem insipid and tame.' The message of this design encourages patriots to support the army by investing in the War Loan and so 'crush England's might'.

"YOUR COUNTRY NEEDS **YOU**"

1914

LORD KITCHENER'S APPEAL

Published by His Majesty's Stationery Office, August 1914

The first government recruiting posters took the form of official printed proclamations informing the public that the country was at war and reminding young men of their patriotic duty to enlist.

At the outbreak of war in August 1914, Britain had a small professional volunteer army of about 250,000 regular troops, almost half of which was stationed overseas in garrisons throughout the British Empire. The regular army was supported by the part-time Territorial Force and by reservists, which had a combined nominal strength of a further 440,000 men. Even so, only 150,000 soldiers were immediately available to be formed into a British Expeditionary Force (BEF) for deployment in France and Flanders. In contrast, France was able to mobilise 1,650,000 troops, while the German Army consisted of almost two million men.

The newly appointed Secretary of State for War, Field Marshal Lord Kitchener (1st Earl Kitchener of Khartoum), was charged with expanding the army to meet the national emergency. Unlike many of his colleagues, Kitchener realised that the war was likely to be a protracted and costly campaign, requiring the formation of the largest army in the nation's history.

His initial request for 100,000 volunteers was quickly met and by the end of August over 300,000 men had joined up.

LORD KITCHENER'S APPEAL.

100,000 Men required for the War.

NO MEN will be REFUSED who are PHYSICALLY FIT for Active Service and between the ages of 19 and 30.

OLD SOLDIERS UP TO 42.

Late N.C.Os. of Regulars and Ex-Soldiers

URGENTLY NEEDED.

Enquire inside for address of nearest Recruiter

30,000 8/14   Printed for His Majesty's Stationery Office by HAZELL, WATSON & VINEY, LD., 52, Long Acre, London, W C

TO ARMS!

Leonard Raven-Hill (1867–1942)
Published by *Punch*, September 1914

In addition to recruiting posters published by the government, many privately owned companies and local organisations printed their own designs in support of the war effort. This poster is based on a cartoon that originally appeared in the satirical magazine *Punch* on 2 September 1914. It depicts the character of Mr Punch, dressed as a recruiting-sergeant, with a government proclamation calling for an additional 500,000 men pasted to the wall in the background.

The artist, Leonard Raven-Hill, was a regular contributor to *Punch* and, together with other well-known pre-war cartoonists and illustrators (including John Hassall, Bernard Partridge, Bert Thomas and Alfred Leete), designed several wartime posters encouraging men to join the armed forces.

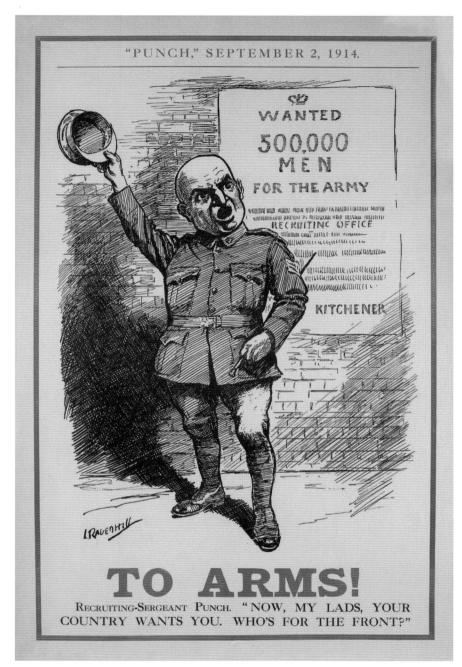

TO ARMS!

RECRUITING-SERGEANT PUNCH. "NOW, MY LADS, YOUR COUNTRY WANTS YOU. WHO'S FOR THE FRONT?"

YOUR COUNTRY NEEDS YOU

Alfred Leete (1882–1933)

Published by *London Opinion*, September 1914

Alfred Leete's striking drawing of Lord Kitchener has become one of the most famous, and most copied, images of the First World War. It was originally designed for the cover of *London Opinion*, a popular illustrated magazine. This poster version was published to advertise the 5 September 1914 edition and would have appeared on news-stands across Britain. The design was so popular that it was turned into a poster in its own right, with the revised wording 'Britons … Wants You' flanking the image of Kitchener.

Despite the poster's enduring popularity, there is some uncertainty as to how widely distributed it was at the time. Other posters featuring Kitchener, or quotes attributed to him, were published in far greater numbers on behalf of the government, whereas the poster based on Leete's design appears to have been privately produced in a limited print run.

Leete was already a very successful illustrator and cartoonist at the start of the war. He regularly contributed to periodicals such as *Punch* and the *Strand Magazine*, and later designed posters for the London Underground, among other clients.

YOUR KING AND COUNTRY NEED YOU

Published by the Parliamentary Recruiting Committee, October 1914

The Parliamentary Recruiting Committee (PRC) was formed at the outset of the war to kick-start the massive recruitment drive needed to expand the army. Chaired by the Prime Minister, Herbert Asquith, this cross-party committee utilised the existing infrastructure in parliamentary constituencies to support recruitment through the distribution of leaflets and posters, and by the organisation of rallies, processions and public meetings.

The first PRC posters, published in September/October 1914, followed a traditional format for official government proclamations, consisting of a concise patriotic message printed beneath the royal monogram. Their official status was reinforced by the use of red and blue text against a white background to imply the colours of the Union Flag.

At this stage in the conflict, many men joined up under the assumption that the war would last only a few months and that it was their duty to volunteer for 'King and Country' until Germany was defeated.

G. R.

YOUR KING
AND
COUNTRY
NEED YOU

JOIN THE ARMY
UNTIL THE
WAR IS OVER

THE SCRAP OF PAPER/
Y "DARN PAPUR"

English and Welsh language versions
Published by the Parliamentary Recruiting Committee, December 1914

Surprisingly few recruiting posters sought to justify the war, but those that did tended to focus on examples of 'Prussian aggression' and duplicity, especially the invasion of 'defenceless' Belgium. The neutrality of the latter had been theoretically guaranteed by the 1839 Treaty of London, signed by the German, French, British and Russian governments (among others). The treaty, contemptuously referred to as 'a scrap of paper' by the Kaiser's Chancellor, was effectively torn up following the invasion on 2 August 1914, which led in turn to Britain's entry into the war.

This perceived act of treachery on Germany's part was widely used in Allied propaganda, even though the treaty had been signed seventy-five years earlier and bore little relevance to the politics of 1914. The posters depicted here were extensively distributed throughout the UK and overseas. The PRC produced Welsh versions of several popular designs, despite the army's pre-war ambivalence to the official use of the language by Welsh regiments.

THE SCRAP OF PAPER

Prussia's Perfidy—Britain's Bond.

The Treaty of 1839 (which the German Chancellor tore up, remarking that it was only "a scrap of paper") said:

"BELGIUM .... SHALL FORM AN INDEPENDENT AND PERPETUALLY NEUTRAL STATE. IT SHALL BE BOUND TO OBSERVE SUCH NEUTRALITY TOWARDS ALL OTHER STATES."

These are the Seals and Signatures of the Six Nations who guaranteed Belgian Independence and Neutrality

GREAT BRITAIN - Palmerston
BELGIUM - Sylvain Van De Weyer
AUSTRIA - Senfft
FRANCE - H. Sebastiani
GERMANY - Bülow
RUSSIA - Pozzo Di Borgo

Germany has trampled on the Treaty she signed.

CAN BRITONS STAND BY WHILE GERMANY CRUSHES AN INNOCENT PEOPLE ?

ENLIST TO-DAY

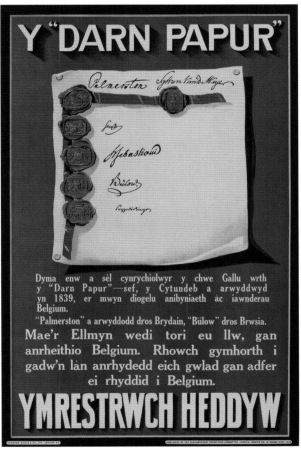

Y "DARN PAPUR"

Dyma enw a sêl cynrychiolwyr y chwe Gallu wrth y "Darn Papur"—sef, y Cytundeb a arwyddwyd yn 1839, er mwyn diogelu anibyniaeth àc iawnderau Belgium.

"Palmerston" a arwyddodd dros Brydain, "Bülow" dros Brwsia.

Mae'r Ellmyn wedi tori eu llw, gan anrheithio Belgium. Rhowch gymhorth i gadw'n làn anrhydedd eich gwlad gan adfer ei rhyddid i Belgium.

YMRESTRWCH HEDDYW

REMEMBER BELGIUM.
ENLIST TO-DAY

Published by the Parliamentary Recruiting Committee, December 1914

In contrast to the sometimes graphic depiction of conflict produced by other combatant nations, British posters rarely showed scenes from the heat of battle. In this oddly passive design, a soldier stands on guard while (in the words of the PRC) 'a woman and her babies are in flight from a blazing home'. The message and image were intended to appeal to the British sense of fair play, reminding un-enlisted men that their duty lay in protecting the victims of German aggression. In so doing the British soldier is presented as heroic and noble compared with his 'barbaric' foe.

Whatever its true merits may have been, 140,000 copies of this poster were printed between December 1914 and March 1915, making it the second most popular image published by the PRC.

REMEMBER BELGIUM

ENLIST TO-DAY

PUBLISHED BY THE PARLIAMENTARY RECRUITING COMMITTEE LONDON. POSTER Nº 19.   W.10054. 25M. 1/15. HENRY JENKINSON LTD KIRKSTALL LEEDS

TO BERLIN!

Published by 4th Battalion, The Buffs, East Kent Regiment, 1914

Not all recruiting posters were serious in their subject matter. This poster was produced locally in Canterbury and aimed to raise recruits for the 4th Battalion, East Kent Regiment, by making light of volunteering. The 4th Battalion was a Territorial Force unit, and ended up spending much of the war in India.

Comparing the war with a hunting trip where accommodation, travel and even ammunition costs would be provided, was designed to appeal to the adventurous, and intended to raise a smile. It highlighted the commonly held belief that the war would be over quickly and easily, culminating in the successful capture of Berlin by spring 1915.

The named recruiter is Private Daniel Sherrin, a local Kent artist who volunteered early in the war. During a recruiting event, he participated in a wager against a local butcher to see if he could paint an oil painting of a yacht on the sea faster than the butcher could carve a roast beef. Sherrin lost by only ten seconds.

TO BERLIN!

The Country is arranging a Trip to Germany in the Spring to a few

SPORTSMEN.

All hotel expenses and railway fares paid.

Good Shooting and Hunting.

Ages 18—38 (?).   Rifles and

AMMUNITION SUPPLIED FREE.

Cheap Trips up the Rhine.

Apply at once as there is only a limited number (one million) required.

APPLY—

PRIVATE DANIEL SHERRIN,
4th Batt. The Buffs,
East Kent Regiment.
Drill Hall,
St. Peter's Lane,
Canterbury.

THE VETERAN'S FAREWELL

Frank Dadd (1851–1929)

Published by the Parliamentary Recruiting Committee, December 1914 (and February 1915)

This traditional image of a new soldier heading off to the front, stopping to shake hands with a Chelsea Pensioner, was first published as a tobacco advertisement for Abdulla & Co and was re-issued by the PRC in black-and-white and colour versions.

The Chelsea Pensioners are retired veterans with long service, and the one depicted here is wearing several campaign medals. The poster implies that Victorian soldiers had done their duty to Britain and it was now time for a new generation to step forward and fulfil their responsibility in a changing of the guard.

Men of fighting age in 1914 grew up learning of the exploits of Victorian soldiers in preceding conflicts through popular publications such as *Boy's Own Paper*, and the martial heroes of that period, such as Lords Roberts, Kitchener and Baden-Powell, were afforded celebrity status in Edwardian Britain.

In the background, a recruiting sergeant is leading a column of new recruits still in civilian clothes, ranging from city workers in pin-striped suits and bowler hats to labourers in workers' dungarees and soft caps, as a visual reminder that men from all walks of life were expected to volunteer.

THE VETERAN'S FAREWELL.

"Good Bye my lad.
I only wish I were young enough
to go with you!"

ENLIST NOW!

OUR ANCESTORS FOUGHT FOR OUR FREEDOM

Bannerman

Published in South Africa, 1914

Although the Union of South Africa was a dominion of the British Empire, war with Germany in 1914 was not universally supported there.

Many South Africans, known as Boers, had German or Dutch ancestry. The use of the Union Flag and the phrase 'Our Ancestors Fought For Our Freedom' would have been divisive, as a large proportion of the population resented the British victory over their short-lived republics in the Second Boer War (1899–1902).

The South African government sided with Britain and declared war on Germany, resulting in plans to invade German South-West Africa. A group of Boer army officers refused to participate and incited a revolt known as the Maritz Rebellion, but it was swiftly crushed.

Prime Minister Louis Botha and Defence Minister General Jan Smuts sought to overcome Boer nationalism by suggesting that the British had actually fought for South Africa's freedom and prosperity, which was growing within the British Empire, and that Germany threatened invasion.

A South African expeditionary force was raised, with over 130,000 men volunteering to serve in both Africa and Europe.

OUR ANCESTORS FOUGHT FOR OUR FREEDOM.

THEN UP BOYS! FIGHT & GUARD IT.

JOIN THE IRISH CANADIAN RANGERS

Published on behalf of the Irish Canadian Rangers, 1914

Upon the outbreak of the First World War, Canada was a loyal part of the British Empire and immediately prepared to send an expeditionary force to aid Britain's war effort.

A large number of emigrants from the British Isles to Canada were Irish, and proudly maintained their Irish identity in Canada. At the time there was a fierce debate over Home Rule for Ireland, but both sides put aside their differences with Nationalist and Unionist leaders backing the war effort. Nationalist leader John Redmond suggested the war effort was also in defence of 'right and freedom', and Irish Catholics were urged to 'save Catholic Belgium'.

Irish Canadians responded to these appeals, leading to the raising of the Irish Canadian Rangers. With a title evoking the famous Connaught Rangers, the Irish Canadian Rangers used Irish symbolism, such as a shamrock cap badge, while the rural idyll depicted in the background is reminiscent of the Irish homeland to appeal to recruits. The 'emigrant sons of Ireland' arrived first in Ireland, where they were popularly received, but before landing in France they were broken up as reinforcements for other units and never fought together.

45

THE ONLY ROAD FOR AN ENGLISHMAN

Gerald Spencer Pryse (1882–1956)

Published by the Underground Electric Railway Company, 1914

London Underground led the way among the many private organisations that published patriotic and recruiting posters during the war. Under the inspired leadership of Frank Pick, the Underground had acquired a well-deserved reputation for the outstanding quality of its peacetime travel posters and now sought to apply the same principles to designing wartime notices. In 1914 Pick actually refused to display the designs of the Parliamentary Recruiting Committee on the Tube because they were 'too bad to be hung'. Instead he commissioned Frank Brangwyn and Gerald Spencer Pryse to create high-quality and memorable designs to encourage commuters to enlist. From 1916 the Underground also commissioned some of the finest artists of the day to produce decorative posters for army billets and YMCA huts as 'a reminder of home'.

  Pryse had initially served as a dispatch rider for the Belgian government and was present at the siege of Antwerp and the battles of the Marne and the Aisne. His first series of wartime lithographs, entitled 'The Autumn Campaign', was published in 1914. Incredibly, Pryce drew the designs directly onto lithographic stones, which he carried in his staff car. He later served as a captain with the King's Royal Rifle Corps and was an official war artist from 1916.

JOHNSON, RIDDLE &C.

Through Darkness
to Light

**THE ONLY ROAD
FOR AN ENGLISHMAN**

Through Fighting
to Triumph

47

REMEMBER SCARBOROUGH!

Published by the Parliamentary Recruiting Committee, December 1914

The German naval raids on the east-coast towns of Scarborough, Hartlepool and Whitby on 16 December 1914 caused public outrage in both Britain and the neutral United States. The attack on Scarborough, in particular, was widely condemned. Famed as a seaside resort with no military significance, the town was defenceless against the long-range guns of the German Imperial Navy. In total, 137 people (many of them civilians) were killed in the combined raids, with a further 592 injured.

Recruitment posters calling on young men to 'avenge Scarborough' were printed within twenty-four hours of the atrocity. The attack was presented as another example of German barbarity, on a par with the treatment of women and children in 'defenceless' Belgium. It was also an unwelcome reminder that the Home Front could be viewed as a legitimate target in the changed circumstances of modern warfare.

REMEMBER SCARBOROUGH!

The Germans who brag of their "CULTURE" have shown what it is made of by murdering defenceless women and children at SCARBOROUGH.

But this only strengthens

GREAT BRITAIN'S
resolve to crush the

GERMAN BARBARIANS

ENLIST NOW!

Published by the Parliamentary Recruiting Committee, 12, Downing Street, London.   Poster No. 29.   Harrison & Sons, Printers, St. Martin's Lane, W.C.

49

1915

REMEMBER! ENGLAND EXPECTS

Henry Lawrence Oakley (1882–1960)
Published on behalf of the Royal Navy, 1915

The recruiting drive of 1914–15 was focused on the rapid, and massive, expansion of the British army to meet the demands of land warfare. In contrast, relatively few posters were produced on behalf of the Royal Navy, although the Admiralty commissioned this design from the silhouette artist Henry Lawrence Oakley in 1915, for which he was paid 10 guineas.

The message is an adaptation of Admiral Nelson's famous signal to the English fleet before the battle of Trafalgar in 1805, 'England expects that every man will do his duty'. Oakley had previously designed a highly successful poster for the Parliamentary Recruiting Committee featuring an advancing soldier in silhouette, and both designs were widely distributed throughout the British Empire.

Oakley later served with the Yorkshire Regiment in France, from where he submitted silhouettes of army life for publication in *The Bystander* magazine. After the war he reopened his portraiture business in Harrogate and Scarborough. Among the many genuine testimonials from satisfied customers displayed in his studio was this spoof supposedly written by the exiled Kaiser in 1919: 'If I had made as good use of Scraps of Paper as you did, there would have been no war' (see *The Scrap of Paper* poster, page 34-5).

HURRY UP! BOYS FILL THE RANKS

John Hassall (1868–1948)

Published on behalf of the Public Schools Brigade, Royal Fusiliers, 1915

One of the great successes of the 1914 recruitment drive had been the formation of so-called 'Pals' Battalions', where neighbours, work colleagues and team mates were encouraged to enlist together. The recruiters rightly suspected that peer pressure and a sense of shared endeavour would overcome individual qualms about joining up.

This poster, by the renowned commercial artist and illustrator John Hassall, is aimed at one such group of 'pals' – ex-public-school boys. Historically, Britain's elite public schools provided the army with officers, rather than private soldiers, but by joining one of the new battalions classmates could serve together in the ranks in the tradition of 'gentlemen volunteers'. Hassall's design emphasises the opportunity for adventure and comradeship offered by this approach, in a style reminiscent of his popular illustrations for children's books. The open-necked shirt and waving gesture, for example, give the soldier a particularly youthful appearance, while the trophies of war strewn at his feet suggest that victory is assured.

The Public Schools Brigade was independently raised in 1914 and later allocated to the Royal Fusiliers as the 18th, 19th, 20th and 21st battalions. By early 1915, when this poster was published, their numbers had been depleted by transfers to other New Army battalions, where public-school graduates were urgently needed to serve as officers.

BRITAIN HAS BEEN ALL SHE COULD BE TO JEWS

Printed on behalf of the Jewish Unit, *c.* 1915

Featuring the Union Flag and the Star of David (*Magen David*), this direct appeal to British Jews repurposes an earlier quote from the *Jewish Chronicle* (August 1914) reminding the Jewish community that Britain had provided a safe haven for around 140,000 Jewish migrants escaping persecution in continental Europe during the nineteenth century.

The militant message was echoed in synagogues, where rabbis encouraged enlistment in their sermons, and Jewish public notables drew parallels between the British war effort and the Jewish cause, to which British Jews responded enthusiastically. Many saw the war as a means to prove their loyalty and counter anti-Semitic charges of selfishness and cowardliness.

Over fifty thousand British Jews responded to the call, and in 1917 an all-Jewish unit called the Jewish Legion was formed. Britain had also recruited the Zion Mule Corps from Jews living in the Middle East and it served in the Gallipoli campaign in 1915. After British Empire forces conquered the Ottoman territory of Palestine in 1917, Zionists in Britain used the loyal service of Jews as the basis for a call to establish a Jewish homeland within Palestine under the terms of the Balfour Declaration.

PLAY THE GREATER GAME

Published by the Central London Recruiting Depot, 1915

This poster features British infantrymen firing from a trench below a vignette of footballers walking out at the start of a match. Above is a condescending quote from the German newspaper *Frankfurter Zeitung*, stating 'The young Britons prefer to exercise their long limbs on the football ground, rather than to expose them to any sort of risk in the service of their country.'

The message was clear: many Germans felt that Britons lacked the resolve to participate in a major European war, and their newspapers used this to bolster self-belief within Germany that the war could be easily won. The German press also interpreted the fact that Britain had to conduct a recruiting campaign in the first place as a sign of national weakness, unnecessary in Germany, where conscription was presented as a national duty.

This poster was, of course, intended to incense British men at the German insult and encourage waverers to join up. Ironically, there was some justification in the taunt, as many professional footballers had initially tried to keep the game going to boost morale. The Football League was eventually suspended from 1915 to 1919.

WOMEN OF BRITAIN SAY – "<u>GO!</u>"

Edgar James Kealey (1889–1977)

Published by the Parliamentary Recruiting Committee, March 1915

Taken at face value, this poster suggests that it is the duty of British women to put aside selfish reasons and encourage their menfolk to enlist. The apparently well-off young woman watching local recruits marching away is accompanied by two refugees – a boy and a girl – thereby implying a dual act of patriotism in both supporting the recruitment drive and offering her home to those escaping persecution on the Continent. But there was more to the image than this. The inclusion of refugees also hints at the implications of a German victory, a prospect made all the more alarming by contemporary newspaper stories regarding the treatment of civilians in occupied Belgium. With this is mind, telling your husband/brother/lover to 'Go' was more that just a duty, it was a matter of self-preservation.

For the eligible recruit targeted by this campaign, the image of vulnerable women stoically seeing off loved ones was also meant to elicit a sense of shame for not having joined up already. The message was reinforced by less subtle recruitment literature, which openly questioned the motivation and manliness of those who chose to stay behind.

WOMEN OF BRITAIN SAY — "GO!"

Published by the PARLIAMENTARY RECRUITING COMMITTEE, London.   Poster No. 75.   Printed by HILL, SIFFKEN & Co. (L.P.A. Ltd.), Grafton Works, London. N.   W.1524C 23 M. 1/15

DADDY, WHAT DID <u>YOU</u> DO IN THE GREAT WAR?

Augustus Savile Lumley (1878–1949)

Published by the Parliamentary Recruiting Committee, March 1915

Set 'about five years after the war' (according to Arthur Gunn, the commercial printer who came up with the idea), the clear message of this disturbing poster is that failure to answer the nation's call now will have life-long repercussions. Children, and especially girls, had long been used in advertising to represent vulnerability and honesty. Here the implication is that the father neither protected his children during the war nor can he hope to win their respect once peace has returned.

The use of emotional bribery to shame young men into volunteering received a mixed response at the time, and is not typical of the majority of posters produced by the British government. Many would-be recruits resented the bullying tone, and serving soldiers made up their own ironic responses to the text of this poster. For others, though, the message had the desired effect. In 1916, for example, Second Lieutenant Douglas Hamlin-Mckie wrote to his fiancée from hospital in Newcastle about his guilt at being kept out of the war due to a leg injury sustained on a cross-country run: 'the idea of "what did you do in the Great War daddy?" – jumped over a fence! Seems rather ridiculous doesn't it?'

Daddy, what did **YOU** do in the Great War?

PUBLISHED BY THE PARLIAMENTARY RECRUITING COMMITTEE, LONDON. POSTER NO. 79.   DESIGNED AND PRINTED BY JOHNSON, RIDDLE & CO., LTD., LONDON, S.E.

63

IF YOU CANNOT JOIN THE ARMY – TRY & GET A RECRUIT

Published by the Parliamentary Recruiting Committee, March 1915

By the beginning of 1915 the numbers of new volunteers had dropped significantly, leading to ever more direct appeals to secure recruits. For the first time posters were addressed not just at potential recruits but also at their families and friends. All were deemed to have an equal responsibility to ensure that every available man was 'doing his bit' for King and Country.

About half of all the recruiting posters published by the government were printed in a text-only format and usually displayed alongside pictorial designs for maximum effect. Over sixty thousand copies of this poster were issued, making it the most widely distributed letterpress design of the PRC's campaign. Like other examples of its type, the poster is printed in red, white and blue to reinforce the patriotic message.

Published by the Parliamentary Recruiting Committee, London   Poster No. 20

THE EMPIRE NEEDS MEN!

Arthur Wardle (1860–1949)

Published by the Parliamentary Recruiting Committee, March 1915

In the late nineteenth and early twentieth centuries, the relationship between Britain and its larger colonies began to evolve and change. Canada had been regarded as a 'dominion' rather than a colony upon its confederation in 1867, and Australia received the same status when it federated in 1901. In 1907 New Zealand and Newfoundland also became dominions, and South Africa joined them in 1910. Along with the Empire of India, the dominions represented the largest, richest and most populous parts of the British Empire.

This poster cleverly shows the British lion defying Germany, but calls on the dominions – represented as lion cubs – to come to Britain's aid. The Barbary lion has been used as a symbol to represent England since the time of King Richard I, 'the Lionheart' (1157–99). Another version was also published, replacing the names of the dominions with 'The Overseas States' to appeal more broadly to the whole Empire.

Despite the growing size of Lord Kitchener's 'New Army', it was recognised that large numbers of men were needed from the dominions as well, and dominion troops had already proved their worth as excellent soldiers in the Boer War (1899–1902). The recruitment of dominion troops proved vital to the war effort and eventual victory – 1,524,187 men from India took up arms, along with 628,964 men from Canada, 416,809 from Australia, 220,099 from New Zealand, 136,070 from South Africa, and 11,922 from Newfoundland.

COME & JOIN THIS HAPPY THRONG

Published by His Majesty's Stationery Office, 1915

This poster was printed in Dublin for the Irish recruiting campaign. It features a large number of Irish soldiers smiling and raising their caps in a welcome to potential new recruits. Despite initial support from both Nationalist and Unionist leaders, recruiting in Ireland was always problematic. Even so, over 200,000 Irishmen joined up from both the Catholic and Protestant communities, collectively suffering over thirty thousand casualties by the war's end.

Recruiting in Ireland was most successful in 1914 and early 1915. But the number of casualties suffered by the 10th Irish Division in Gallipoli in 1915 badly affected Irish recruitment and, when Pope Benedict XV condemned the war in July 1915, Roman Catholics began withdrawing their support. Reports also filtered back to Ireland of Irish soldiers receiving unfair treatment from their British commanders.

By the middle of 1915 recruiting was no longer providing enough volunteers from across the whole United Kingdom. The Military Service Act 1916 introduced conscription for England, Scotland and Wales, but Ireland was exempt because of the declining support for the war effort there. The ongoing debate over Home Rule and the religious and geographic divisions within Ireland also lingered in the background, eventually leading to the Easter Rising of April 1916. Prior to the Rising these differences were largely overlooked, but that event shook and re-shaped Ireland and its relationship with the United Kingdom for ever.

BOYS COME OVER HERE YOU'RE WANTED

Published by the Parliamentary Recruiting Committee, March 1915

By January 1915 over a million men had enlisted to bolster the waning strength of British forces at the front. During fighting in 1914 and early 1915, the British Army had suffered over ninety thousand casualties, and new recruits were continually required, leading to the title of this poster – *Boys Come over here you're wanted*. It was printed by David Allen & Sons, who produced around a quarter of all PRC posters during the war.

This distinctive poster alludes to the custom of representing Britain and its Empire on maps with pink, a practice that began in the nineteenth century. In front of the map, a fit young British soldier in pristine khaki-coloured Service Dress uniform and 1908 Pattern web equipment, with Short Magazine Lee Enfield rifle in hand, peers across the Channel from France to England 'looking' for more recruits. He also wears a single chevron, denoting a lance corporal, suggesting he has already gained some experience.

The following month, another version with the soldier in silhouette was also published, and a slightly different version was also released, entitled *Come Lad Slip Across and Help*, in which a soldier in uniform helps a civilian to hop across the channel to join him.

YOUR COUNTRY'S CALL. ISN'T THIS WORTH FIGHTING FOR? ENLIST NOW

Published by the Parliamentary Recruiting Committee, April 1915

With the Kaiser's army poised near the English Channel and the invasion of Belgium fresh in the popular consciousness, posters such as *Your Country's Call* highlighted the real threat to the British way of life posed by a German victory. As in the Second World War, idyllic depictions of rural England, somewhat incongruously guarded here by a Highland soldier, reminded both would-be recruits and the families of enlisted men of the reasons Britain was at war.

Of course, the majority of soldiers came from industrial and urban regions, but it was the idealised version of a peaceful land of quiet villages and rolling hills that dominated wartime propaganda, providing a sharp contrast to the reality of life in the trenches.

Although the Scottish soldier at first appears out of place among the thatched cottages and dovecots, Highlanders actually featured in a number of recruitment posters to highlight the sense of national unity and regional colour. The PRC even put together a touring Highland Pipe Band, which visited over 650 towns, cities and villages between November 1914 and February 1916.

YOUR COUNTRY'S CALL

Isn't this worth fighting for?
ENLIST NOW

PUBLISHED BY THE PARLIAMENTARY RECRUITING COMMITTEE, LONDON.   POSTER Nº 87.   PRINTED BY JOWETT & SOWRY, LEEDS.

WHY BOTHER ABOUT THE GERMANS INVADING THE COUNTRY?

The Brothers Warbis

Published by the Underground Electric Railway Company, 1915

At first, the war made little impact on the day-to-day lives of those who remained in Britain. Railway companies, including London Underground, continued to advertise leisure travel, even though many trains were overcrowded with soldiers returning to and from the front line. Perhaps unsurprisingly, posters promoting day trips and holidays to a war-weary public seldom made reference to the fighting overseas. This striking exception, encouraging Londoners to 'invade' the country for themselves, was published by the Underground Group (which included the General bus company) in Easter 1915.

Growing fuel shortages and a general tightening of wartime restrictions eventually led to official discouragement of pleasure trips by public transport – an approach the government was later to adopt from the outset of the Second World War.

WHY BOTHER ABOUT THE
GERMANS INVADING
THE COUNTRY?

INVADE IT YOURSELF
BY **Underground** AND MOTOR-'BUS

EASTER · 1915

SURELY YOU WILL FIGHT FOR YOUR [KING] AND [COUNTRY]?

Published by the Parliamentary Recruiting Committee, May 1915

Parliamentary Recruiting Committee posters invariably addressed the viewer as a dutiful citizen unquestioningly loyal to King and Country. Representations of King George V and/or the British Isles were regularly deployed to elicit a suitable patriotic response, as was the phrase 'Come along, boys' with its paternalistic, slightly school-masterly tone.

Certainly many of the one million recruits who joined up between August 1914 and January 1915 did so out of a genuine and deep-seated sense of national duty that pre-dated the start of the war. Indeed, it is important to remember that successful posters and recruitment literature did not manufacture consent, but rather they appealed to pre-existing beliefs and attitudes.

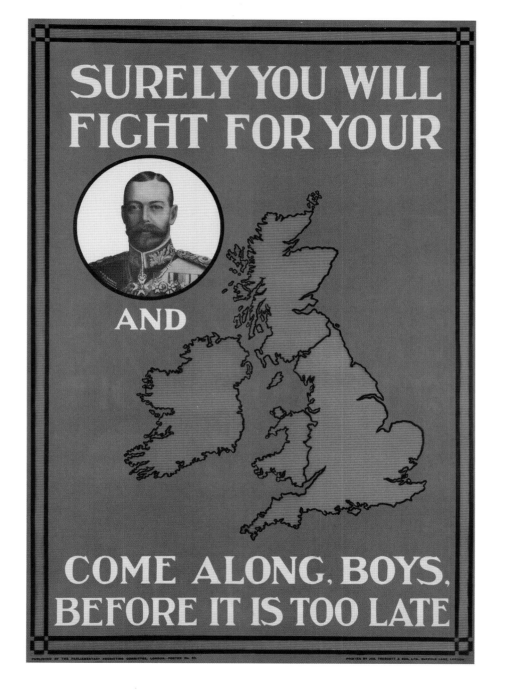

WHICH OUGHT <u>YOU</u> TO WEAR?

Published by the Central London Recruiting Depot, May 1915

As the war progressed and voluntary recruitment dipped, an increasing number of posters sought to shame young men into enlisting. In this design, commissioned by the Central London Recruitment Depot, a khaki service cap is contrasted favourably with a range of hats associated with peacetime employment and leisure pursuits, suggesting that the un-enlisted male civilian has a duty to join up rather than carrying on his pre-war lifestyle. The point was explicitly, if rather bizarrely, made in an associated press statement, which explained: 'The man we want to get at is the young slacker with "cold feet" who goes about town in a straw hat and fancy socks.' The government, too, was worried that 'slackers' were letting others carry the burden of the fighting, and published its own version of this poster with the words, 'If the cap fits You, join the army To-day'.

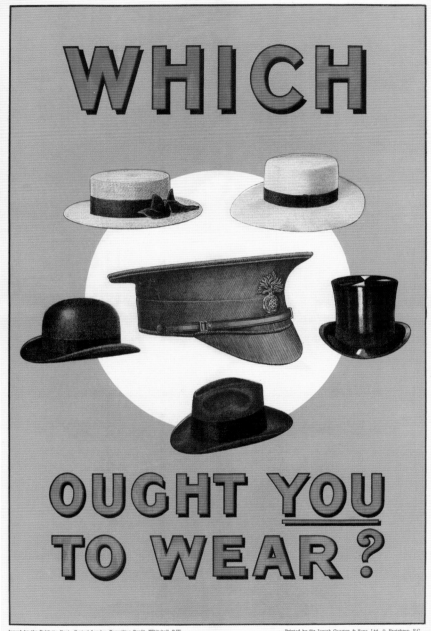

Issued by the Publicity Dept. Central London Recruiting Depôt. Whitehall. S.W.   Printed by Sir Joseph Causton & Sons. Ltd., 9, Eastcheap. E.C.

WE'RE BOTH NEEDED TO SERVE THE GUNS!

Published by the Parliamentary Recruiting Committee, May 1915

Government recruiting posters usually implied, or actually stated outright, that the only legitimate role for a young man during the war was to join his comrades in the army, but in this image a munitions worker is given equal status to a soldier under the slogan 'We're both needed to serve the guns'. To emphasise the point, a factory is shown in the background connected by rail to the front line, where a battle is in progress.

The poster was directly commissioned by the PRC (unlike the majority of speculatively submitted designs), apparently at the request of the War Office. The shift in focus to 'war work' was almost certainly the result of the 'shell crisis' of early 1915, when a shortage of high-explosive artillery rounds was widely blamed in the press for the failure of recent British offensives. The crisis led to the appointment of David Lloyd George as Minister of Munitions and to legislation to increase production.

Over 100,000 copies of this poster were printed in various sizes – testimony to the importance placed on its message by the government. 'Heads of industrial municipalities' were instructed to display the largest version (10 feet by 6 feet 8 inches) on specially erected hoardings at 'central spots', where the design was apparently well received – probably because of its more inclusive tone. The London correspondent of the *Manchester Courier,* for example, claimed: 'It is perhaps the most effective placard that has yet been issued and its exhibition in prominent places throughout the industrial district should lead not only to successful recruitment but to an increase in the production of munitions' (12 May 1915).

STEP INTO YOUR PLACE

Published by the Parliamentary Recruiting Committee, May 1915

In Britain, recruitment propaganda often presented the transformation from civilian to military life as a seamless transition. Little reference was made to the harsh, and sometimes brutal, regime of the army with its emphasis on unbending rules, discipline and occasional punishment. Similarly, there was little or no suggestion that active service entailed a very real risk of injury or death. Instead posters emphasised the communal nature of wartime experience, with men from all social classes and professions answering the call together.

The range of identifiable 'types' depicted in this poster, from office workers to labourers and lawyers, would have been well understood by contemporaries, and shows the influence of pre-war advertising techniques that stressed the importance of the 'consumer' (in this case the would-be recruit) being able to identify with the 'product' (i.e. enlistment).

STEP INTO YOUR PLACE

PUBLISHED BY THE PARLIAMENTARY RECRUITING COMMITTEE, LONDON — POSTER N° 104   PRINTED BY DAVID ALLEN & SONS L™, HARROW MIDDLESEX. W 5846 4014

"SEND MORE MEN!"

Norman Keene

Published on behalf of the 23rd and 24th Battalions, Royal Fusiliers, 1915

This poster features a wounded dispatch rider, complete with Douglas motorcycle, pointing to a burning village in the distance in an effort to encourage more 'sportsmen' to enlist.

The demands of soldiering required a high degree of strength and fitness and not everyone eligible was suitable, and so natural athletes, sportsmen and sporting shooters were obvious targets for recruiting. The 1914 drive for men of all classes to fill the ranks of Lord Kitchener's 'New Army' had seen sportsmen particularly encouraged to form 'Pals' Battalions', and many cricket, rugby and football teams, such as Clapton Orient (now Leyton Orient), joined en masse.

By mid-1915, with recruit numbers falling, a fresh appeal for athletic men was needed. Posters like this one, featuring a motorcycle, were intended to appeal to sporting types, drawn to the excitement of fast machines and motor sports. It was aimed at raising recruits for the 23rd and 24th (Service) Battalions, Royal Fusiliers, known as the 1st and 2nd Sportsmen's Battalions, which recruited from the Hotel Cecil in London. The 1st Sportsmen were also known as the 'Hard as Nails Battalion', and earned fame for their actions at Delville Wood during the Battle of the Somme in 1916.

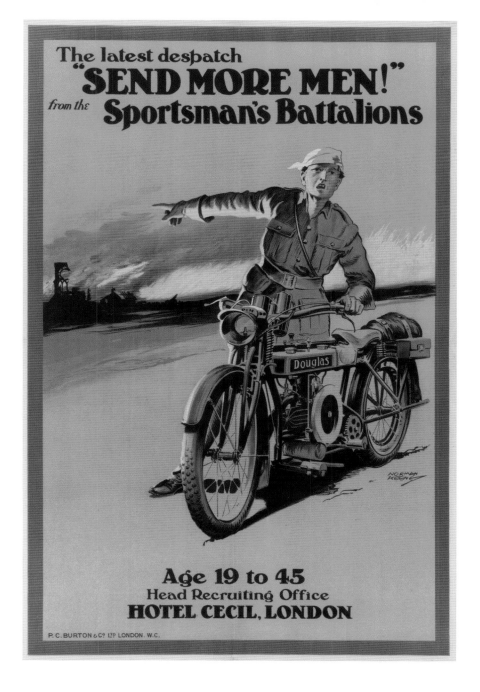

TAKE UP THE SWORD OF JUSTICE

Bernard Partridge (1861–1945)

Published by the Parliamentary Recruiting Committee, June 1915

This dramatic image refers to the sinking of the transatlantic liner *Lusitania*, which was torpedoed off the coast of Ireland in May 1915 by a German U-boat. The ship was returning to Liverpool from New York with almost two thousand passengers on board, nearly 1,200 of whom were drowned.

The incident caused an international outcry, although the German government had declared its intention to sink all British shipping a few months earlier and had even taken out advertisements in American newspapers warning passengers not to travel. Controversy raged as to whether the ship was a legitimate target as it was carrying munitions destined for British troops.

Partridge's painterly design features a heroic depiction of Britannia offering the viewer the 'sword of justice' with which to avenge the dead. The poster was favourably reviewed at the time, with the *London Evening Express* concluding: 'it is a very effective picture, calculated to appeal alike to the artistic and patriotic.' With 105,000 copies eventually printed, this was one of the most widely seen posters of the war.

TAKE UP THE SWORD OF JUSTICE

PUBLISHED BY THE PARLIAMENTARY RECRUITING COMMITTEE, LONDON — POSTER No 105   PRINTED BY DAVID ALLEN & SONS Ltd, HARROW, MIDDLESEX. W. 591. 25M. 6/15

IT IS FAR BETTER TO FACE THE BULLETS THAN TO BE KILLED AT HOME BY A BOMB

Published by the Central London Recruiting Depot, 1915

Regional recruiting agencies mixed civil pride with local concerns to encourage enlistment, as in this example published by the Central London Recruiting Depot which exploits the fear of aerial attack while simultaneously suggesting that the best way to protect the city from further damage is by joining up. The poster, which features a German Zeppelin airship caught in the beam of a searchlight, is also intended to shame the undecided by implying that their motivation to stay at home is based on a misplaced belief in the safety of civilian life.

The first air raids on the capital in May 1915 had caused considerable panic and, like the shelling of Scarborough a few months earlier, demonstrated that the Home Front was no longer a safe haven from the war. In the months that followed, fifty further Zeppelin raids took place and a blackout was imposed on the city.

IT IS FAR BETTER TO FACE THE BULLETS THAN TO BE KILLED AT HOME BY A BOMB

JOIN THE ARMY AT ONCE & HELP TO STOP AN AIR RAID

GOD SAVE THE KING

ISSUED BY THE PUBLICITY DEPARTMENT, CENTRAL RECRUITING DEPOT, WHITEHALL, S.W.   ANDREW REID & CO., LTD., 50, GREY STREET, NEWCASTLE-ON-TYNE.

BRITAIN NEEDS YOU AT ONCE

Published by the Parliamentary Recruiting Committee, June 1915

ZEICHNET-DIE-SECHSTE KRIEGSANLEIHE

Maximilian Lenz (1860–1948)
Published by the Austrian government, 1917

The image of St George slaying the dragon, seen here in a British recruiting poster and an Austrian War Loans design, was used by both sides to symbolise the ultimate triumph of good over evil and reflects the cultural heritage of the combatant European nations. It also represented the values of an imagined medieval past, popularised in England by the Arts and Crafts Movement and illustrated children's literature, which emphasised the chivalry and nobility of combat.

How far removed this romanticised view of warfare was from the realities of the Western Front can easily be imagined. Even so, depictions of armoured warriors fighting for justice and honour recur in the propaganda literature of many of the combatant countries, whether in the form of national symbols such as Britannia (Great Britain), Marianne (France) and Liberty (USA) or as heroes from the past. The use of medieval knights to represent national virtues was especially popular in Germany and Austria, where such images drew on a rich tradition of folklore and historical fact.

TURN YOUR SILVER INTO BULLETS

Published by the Parliamentary War Savings Committee, 1915

From 1914 it was clear that the British government could not finance the war from normal revenue. The conflict was estimated to cost £1 million a day, and alternative sources of funding, including the sale of Treasury Bills, were urgently pursued. In November the government launched the first of three interest-bearing War Loans to encourage the public to lend money to the state. The scheme was extended in 1917 with the introduction of War Bonds, often targeted to support specific fund-raising campaigns.

The resulting publicity campaign was managed by the Parliamentary War Savings Committee from June 1915. Subscribing to War Loans and Bonds was presented as both a patriotic act and an indicator of faith in Britain's ultimate victory.

This poster is for the Second War Loan introduced in June 1915, which offered investors a guaranteed interest rate of 4.5 per cent. Hedley Le Bas, who also advised the government on its recruiting campaign, was given the task of selling the loan. In explaining his approach, Le Bas reasoned that 'we must give the investor something for nothing to make him lend his money. In other words, why not make patriotism profitable?'

The dual appeal to patriotism and profitability is evident here through the gesture of handing over savings to be turned into bullets and by the inclusion of a 5s War Loan voucher (known as a 'silver bullet') guaranteeing a healthy return on investment.

93

WHO CAN BEAT THIS PLUCKY FOUR?

Published by the Department of Recruiting for Ireland, June 1915

This poster invokes the perceived strength in unity of the four constituent nations of the United Kingdom in 1915 – England, Ireland, Scotland and Wales. It features British soldiers from all four countries, each with his national flag attached to his bayonet.

Kneeling at the left is an English soldier with the royal arms of England – three gold lions passant on a red field. In the centre is a Scottish Highlander in a kilt and glengarry cap, with the royal arms of Scotland – a red lion rampant on a yellow field. The right-hand kneeling soldier is Welsh, flying a slightly inaccurate flag representing the arms of the principality of Wales.

Standing to the rear is the Irish soldier, seeming to come to the aid of the other three, and flying the Green Harp flag, associated with Irish identity. Its colours of green and orange were intended to represent Irish unity between Roman Catholics and Protestants. The green, white and orange tricolour that became the Irish national flag in 1919 was considered unacceptable by Loyalists at the time.

This poster was published only in Ireland, and was clearly intended to appeal to those in support of remaining fully within the United Kingdom. The defensive posture of the soldiers reminds potential Irish recruits that the British Army is made up of soldiers from all four nations, and that unity is the basis of their strength.

WHO CAN BEAT THIS PLUCKY FOUR?

BUT ALL THE SAME WE'RE WANTING MORE

JAMES WALKER (Dublin) L.ᵈ DUBLIN.

W.T.P. 47. 7,500 6/15

GO! IT'S YOUR DUTY LAD.
JOIN TO-DAY

Published by the Parliamentary Recruiting Committee, June 1915

Whereas earlier government recruiting literature had reminded young women of their duty to encourage loved ones to enlist, this poster appeals directly to mothers to put aside selfish reasons and ensure that their sons heed the call. It was not a popular design, partly because of its hectoring tone, but also because of its similarity with contemporary commercial advertising, which was becoming an increasingly resented feature of the PRC's campaign.

The bold background colour and use of a central figure to point out the message could have been used to advertise one of a dozen popular brands, as critics noted at the time. A spoof version of this poster appeared in *The Bystander* magazine (8 September 1915) with the alternative wording: 'For a 19/9d Suit, of Nutty distinction and cut by masters of the Sartorial art, GO to……..'

The problem lay in the way new designs were created by commercial printers on behalf of the government with little, or no, official guidance. Inevitably, this led advertisers to deploy well-worn and familiar methods of persuasion, which ultimately served to alienate potential recruits. As the *Daily Mail* commented in April 1915, 'advertising for people to go to the war [has become] just like advertising for people to buy a popular cigarette or a new boot polish'.

The public reaction to the inappropriateness of this approach caused alarm at the War Office, where a more direct appeal to patriotism and duty was preferred. It was also blamed for contributing to the decline in voluntary enlistment, which in turn raised questions about the effectiveness of the PRC's methods.

GO !

IT'S YOUR
DUTY LAD

JOIN TO-DAY

PUBLISHED BY THE PARLIAMENTARY RECRUITING COMMITTEE LONDON. POSTER N°109

ARE YOU IN THIS?

Lieutenant-General Sir Robert Baden-Powell (1857–1941)

Published by the Parliamentary Recruiting Committee, July 1915

Despite growing resentment from the public and serving soldiers, government recruitment posters continued to mix patriotism with guilt to encourage enlistment. In this design, by former Boer War (1899–1902) hero and founder of the Boy Scout movement, Sir Robert Baden-Powell, a cross-section of society is depicted united in the war effort, with the exception of a young man in civilian dress who is, by implication, a 'slacker' avoiding his patriotic responsibilities. In an unambiguous slur on the type of men who failed to answer the nation's call, the 'slacker' is represented as being physically less manly than his male counterparts serving in the armed forces or working in the foundries, and less useful than the Boy Scout, nurse and munitions worker who are all 'in this' together.

By the summer of 1915 there were signs that enthusiasm for the war was flagging. Recruitment in Britain fell from 135,000 in May to just 95,000 in July. Officials at the War Office began to question the effectiveness of the PRC campaign, claiming that the target audience was 'sick of posters and recruitment meetings.' Local demand had certainly fallen away and by July 1915 an estimated one million stockpiled recruiting posters remained undistributed, resulting in a temporary suspension of new orders.

DESIGNED BY LT GEN SIR R.S.S. BADEN POWELL.

Are <u>YOU</u> in this?

PUBLISHED BY THE PARLIAMENTARY RECRUITING COMMITTEE, LONDON.—POSTER NO.112.

PRINTED BY JOHNSON, RIDDLE & CO., LTD., LONDON, S.E.

LORD KITCHENER SAYS... ENLIST TO-DAY

Published by the Parliamentary Recruiting Committee, July 1915

As Secretary of State for War, the hugely popular Lord Kitchener came to epitomise the national war effort. By 1916 the practice of recruiting by posters was known as a 'Kitchener Campaign' in the United States and even those who did not admire Kitchener as a military leader (and there were several in the War Cabinet) recognised his organisational flair. Lady Asquith, the wife of the Prime Minister, famously called him a 'poor general but a wonderful poster', and there can be little doubt that many enlisted because of the recruitment programme he put in place.

This poster uses a pre-war photograph of Kitchener taken by the society photographer Alexander Bassano and includes quotes from a speech delivered at the Guildhall in London on 9 July 1915 calling on men to enlist voluntarily now rather than wait for compulsory conscription to be introduced later. David Allen & Sons printed 145,000 copies on behalf of the PRC during July and August – the largest print run for any of the recruiting posters published by the government.

Kitchener's untimely death in June 1916 was greeted as a national tragedy. He was drowned en route to Russia when his ship, HMS *Hampshire*, struck a mine off the west coast of the Orkney Islands.

101

THERE'S ROOM FOR YOU. ENLIST TO-DAY

W. A. Fry

Published by the Parliamentary Recruiting Committee, August 1915

This is another of the many PRC posters calling on 'YOU' to enlist today, reinforced by the pointing figures of happy soldiers on their way to the front. The only person left behind on the platform is an elderly man clearly too old to fight. The message was reiterated from every hoarding, with related posters aimed at mothers and fiancées asking: '[is] your best boy in khaki?'

Such images helped to foster the idea that all young men not in uniform must, by implication, be 'shirkers' or 'slackers' – a view powerfully expressed by the practice of handing white feathers to men in civilian clothes as a badge of dishonour. Patriotic newspapers, however, drew a distinction between the 'rejected heroes' who had tried and failed to enlist (usually on medical grounds) and those who chose not to join up for 'selfish reasons'. According to the *Evening Telegraph and Post* (10 June 1915), the latter has 'skin as thick as an elephant. Nothing can move him. He's not going. It has never even occurred to him that he is expected to go. It is not him that the poster underlines the word YOU for, it's the other fellow.'

THERE'S ROOM FOR YOU

ENLIST TO-DAY

PUBLISHED BY THE PARLIAMENTARY RECRUITING COMMITTEE, LONDON. POSTER No.122

PRINTED BY WM. STRAIN & SONS, LTD., BELFAST; AND 105 HIGH HOLBORN, LONDON, W.C.

WAR LOAN. BACK THE EMPIRE WITH YOUR SAVINGS. INVEST NOW.

Published by the Parliamentary War Savings Committee, 1915

As with the government's recruiting campaign, the majority of posters published on behalf of the PWSC were designed on the initiative of local printers rather than being directly commissioned. This anonymous design uses the familiar image of the British lion to attract support for the Second War Loan, in a poster that bears a striking similarity to Arthur Wardle's *The Empire Needs Men!* A clear link is made between supporting the War Loan and supporting the empire, suggesting that Britain's position as a world power is at risk if funds are not forthcoming to win the war.

The amount raised by government loans and bonds increased steadily in the second half of the war as wages rose but opportunities to spend contracted because of wartime shortages. *Punch* magazine, however, resented 'the universal eruption of posters imploring us to subscribe to the War Loan' (August 1915), believing that it was another example of the government seeking to control public opinion through the use of advertising agencies and techniques.

WAR LOAN

BACK THE
EMPIRE
WITH YOUR
SAVINGS

APPLY FOR
DETAILS
AT NEAREST
POST
OFFICE.

INVEST NOW

PUBLISHED BY THE PARLIAMENTARY WAR SAVINGS COMMITTEE, LONDON. POSTER Nº 21.   PRINTERS SIR JOSEPH CAUSTON & SONS, LIMITED, LONDON.

HEROES OF ST JULIEN AND FESTUBERT

Published in Canada, *c.* 1915–16

The use of national symbols was common in recruiting posters published in all of the dominions of the British Empire. In this poster a Canadian soldier stands to attention before a Union Flag bordered with Canada's national symbol, the maple leaf, the use of which dates back to the French colony of New France in the eighteenth century.

This poster was produced in English and French versions and evokes the sacrifice of the Canadians who suffered terrible casualties during the dual battles of St Julien and Festubert in April and May 1915, as part of the wider Second Battle of Ypres. The Canadians sustained over six thousand casualties – a third of the First Canadian Division, but still managed to achieve most of their objectives, including capturing the town of Festubert and securing the reputation of the Canadians as capable soldiers.

The bold statement at the bottom – 'Shall We Follow Their Example?' – is a clear evocation that the reputation won by those heroes of St Julien and Festubert was in need of protection by additional recruits.

HEROES OF St.JULIEN AND FESTUBERT

Here's to the Soldier who bled
To the Sailor that bravely did fa.'
Their fame is alive, though their spirits have fled
On the wings of the Year that's awa.'

SHALL WE FOLLOW THEIR EXAMPLE?
APPLY AT RECRUITING STATION

Printed by GAZETTE PRINTING CO. LIMITED, Montreal, Canada

WHO'S ABSENT? IS IT <u>YOU?</u>

Published by the Parliamentary Recruiting Committee, September 1915

Since the eighteenth century the figure of John Bull, with his distinctive Union Flag waistcoat and portly demeanour, had been used to personify perceived British, and especially English, values. Invariably portrayed as honest, direct, patriotic and suspicious of foreigners, it was inevitable that his image and spirit would be evoked for recruiting purposes in 1914–15.

In an echo of Alfred Leete's portrayal of Lord Kitchener, Bull is shown here pointing directly at the viewer and asking whether it is 'you' who are absent. Several other PRC posters adopted a similar approach, emphasising the role of the individual and often including spaces in the ranks (as here) to be filled. Unusually, the line-up does not feature the cheery recruits typical of comparable images. Instead, some of the soldiers (one of whom is hatless) appear to have come straight from combat, suggested by burning buildings, in a rare allusion to the actual fighting.

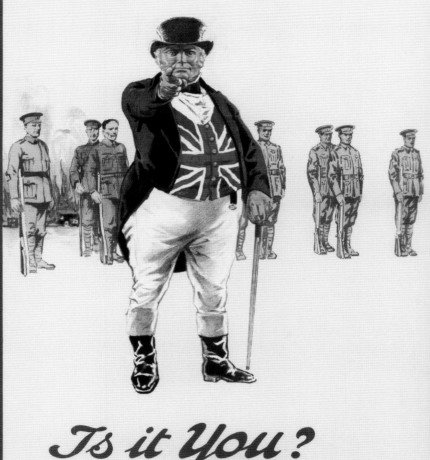

WHO'S ABSENT?

Is it You?

PUBLISHED BY THE PARLIAMENTARY RECRUITING COMMITTEE, LONDON. POSTER No. 125.   PRINTED BY ANDREW REID & CO. LTD., 50, GREY STREET, NEWCASTLE-ON-TYNE

COME NOW. BE HONEST WITH YOURSELF

'P.J.W.'

Published by the Parliamentary Recruiting Committee, September 1915

Lord Kitchener's famous quote, 'Be honest with yourself. Be certain that your so-called reason is not a selfish excuse', was first used in Soutril's well-known silhouetted poster of an artillery crew using a spotter and aircraft to search for enemy locations. The quote was subsequently reused in full or part in several other posters, such as in this example with an additional message to the viewer, that 'Your arms uniform and accoutrements are ready waiting for you'.

This simple poster design features a British soldier's uniform and equipment of the early war hanging from pegs. It includes a khaki Service Dress uniform of olive-drab serge tunic, trousers and greatcoat, a 1905 Pattern Service Dress cap, 1908 Pattern web equipment (ammunition pouches and haversack), and a .303 Short Magazine Lee Enfield rifle and bayonet. On the floor are 'ammunition boots' and rolled puttees. The poster suggests that the government has done its bit in providing the right equipment, and now it is up to the recruit to do his.

THE "STUDINGTON" MILITARY KIT

Published by Studd & Millington, 1915

Other ranks had uniforms provided, but officers had to purchase their own from private tailors, such as Studd & Millington, who had outlets in London and the south-east.

Officers were expected to wear khaki open-collar jackets, shirt and tie, tan jodhpur-style cord breeches, leather trench boots, and leather gloves. They would also wear a Sam Browne shoulder and waist belt with compass and binoculars cases, a map and notebook case, and a pistol holster. Enterprising suppliers designed all manner of unnecessary add-ons to increase cost.

The colour and quality of officers' uniforms varied greatly according to social class, wealth and geography – many different providers meant a large degree of variation. Jacket colours strayed from olive green to brown, and shirts were accepted in khaki, olive, tan and brown, but senior officers complained about junior officers wearing mustard or yellow shirts.

Initially officers' ranks were indicated by braid, crowns and pips on pointed cuff flaps, as shown here, but this was found to attract enemy sniper-fire. In 1915, some officers began wearing rank insignia on their shoulder epaulettes instead. Initially frowned upon, it was officially adopted in 1917.

Selling uniforms and provisions to sometimes quite wealthy officers was very tempting to commercial providers. Catalogues and posters were used to attract sales, with some products (such as Fortnum & Mason's luxurious Christmas hamper) being available for delivery direct to the Western Front.

FORWARD TO VICTORY

Lucy Kemp-Welch (1869–1958)

Published by the Parliamentary Recruiting Committee, September 1915

This was the PRC's last pictorial poster. By September 1915 it was clear that voluntary enlistment would not be sufficient – that month saw only 72,000 new recruits. Moreover, the public was clearly tired of government campaigns and resistant to the commercially inspired hard sell deployed in posters, and so the War Office came to see PRC poster campaigns as a waste of public money. In October the newly appointed Director General of Recruitment, Lord Derby, declared that 'pictorial posters had had their day', and concentrated on letterpress notices outlining the changes to voluntary recruitment and the introduction of conscription from January 1916. No longer needed for recruiting purposes, the PRC was merged with the Parliamentary War Savings Committee to raise funds for the war effort.

During its short existence the PRC printed almost 13 million posters and window cards in 164 designs, plus 34 million leaflets and 5.5 million pamphlets. Its failure to sustain enlistment rates was partly due to public awareness that the war would be more protracted than first thought, but the PRC had also lacked a strategy to bend the designs to popular sentiment: this charging cavalryman, for example, was laughably outdated to a nation aware of the realities of trench warfare.

Even so, 2.5 million British men had joined up in the first sixteen months of the war, no doubt partly inspired by PRC posters.

1916

MEN OF SOUTH AFRICA AVENGE

Bert Thomas (1883–1966)
Published in South Africa, 1916

Men of South Africa Avenge depicts a South African soldier bugler summoning support as he kneels over the body of a prostrate Red Cross nurse on a grassy hillside. She is intended to represent British-born Edith Cavell, who lived in Belgium prior to the war, working as a matron in a training school for student nurses. When the war began she remained in Belgium, giving up her school to the Red Cross. She worked for them treating the wounded of both sides without distinction or favour.

However, in November 1914 Cavell also began aiding Entente soldiers to escape from German-occupied Belgium into neutral Holland. In August 1915 the Germans arrested her and charged her with 'aiding a hostile power'. Although medical personnel were entitled to protection under the Geneva Convention, that protection could be forfeited by any belligerent action.

Cavell confessed in her trial and was sentenced to execution by firing squad, which was carried out on 12 October 1915. The execution of a nurse caused outrage across the British Empire and in the United States. Because public opinion about the war was divided in South Africa, any event that could turn opinion against Germany, such as Cavell's execution, was quickly seized as propaganda to highlight German barbarism and ruthlessness.

WOUNDED ALLIES DAYS AT THE CALEDONIAN MARKET ISLINGTON

Leopold Pilichowski (1869–1934)

Published by the Wounded Allies Relief Committee, June 1916

Formed in 1914, the Wounded Allies Relief Committee (WARC) was one of many charitable bodies created during the war to provide assistance for disabled servicemen and civilians displaced by the conflict. Although independent of government control, the resulting publicity campaigns and fund-raising events helped to secure popular support for the war and effectively supplemented official efforts. Several notable artists, including Frank Brangwyn, John Hassall and, in this case, Leopold Pilichowski, waived their usual fees to provide promotional artwork, which was widely distributed in the form of pamphlets, flags and posters. The National Committee for the Relief of Belgium, for example, published 185,000 posters in 1915 alone.

Like similar charities, the WARC was well-connected, with serving members including the retailer Gordon Selfridge and the writer Arnold Bennett. At first the Committee's efforts were focused on finding families willing to take in wounded Belgian soldiers evacuated to England. By 1916 the charity's remit had expanded to include the provision of hospitals in France and elsewhere, and financial support for the Belgian, French and Serbian Red Cross. The fund-raising event referred to in this poster was a two-day jumble sale and auction held at the Caledonian Road market in Islington, north London. According to a contemporary account, the donated articles on sale 'ranged from an elephant to postcards'. One stall, staffed by Lady Paget and the actress Ellen Terry, raised over £1,000.

YOUR PLACE IS WITH YOUR CHUMS

David Turner

Published by the Department of Recruiting for Ireland, 1916

Without conscription, recruiters in Ireland continued to rely on poster campaigns for longer than they did within the rest of the United Kingdom.

Unlike the poster *Who Can Beat This Plucky Four?* (1915), which was aimed at Irish Loyalists, this poster takes a broader perspective on duty. It features a sergeant of the Royal Irish Regiment saluting the flags of all the Entente powers – Serbia, Russia, France, the United Kingdom, Belgium, Japan and Montenegro.

The Irish Green Harp flag is symbolically placed in the centre of the Entente war effort. By including the flags of allied nations, this poster distances recruitment from being Anglo-centric, making the appeal seem an international one.

The brutal and swift punishment of the Easter Rising rebels in 1916 had turned large sections of the Irish public against England and the Union, and certainly against fighting a 'British imperial war'. With five hundred killed and the ringleaders executed, support for the war effort effectively collapsed in Ireland. Nationalists increasingly saw the war as an imperial conflict and vocally opposed recruitment.

An attempt was made in 1918 to introduce Irish conscription, but it was met with widespread opposition and even unrest. The 1918 elections resulted in a landslide victory in Ireland for the pro-Home Rule party Sinn Féin and in 1919 they declared Irish independence. But disagreements between Unionists and Nationalists escalated into the Irish War of Independence (1919–21), and subsequent Irish Civil War (1922–3).

IF YOU ARE AN IRISHMAN YOUR PLACE IS WITH YOUR CHUMS UNDER THE FLAGS.

David Allen & Sons Ltd. 40, Gt. Brunswick St. Dublin.

123

ENLIST IN THE SPORTSMEN'S 1000

Published in Australia, 1916

At the beginning of the war, Australian volunteers came forward in such numbers that many were turned away. High casualty rates and accounts of the realities of the front caused numbers to drop off, as they had done in the United Kingdom.

When the United Kingdom introduced conscription, Australia's Labor Prime Minister, Billy Hughes, also attempted to adopt it, but two referenda in October 1916 and November 1917 rejected it. Australia and South Africa were the only belligerents on either side remaining entirely voluntary during the First World War. Therefore Australia continued its drive for recruits through recruiting campaigns longer than the United Kingdom.

This poster featured Albert Jacka, Australia's first Victoria Cross recipient in the war. He was an archetypal 'Aussie' sportsman, and had been a successful boxer before the war. 'Sportsmen's battalions' had enjoyed some early success in the United Kingdom, but by 1915 they lost effectiveness as most men willing to volunteer had done so. In Australia, by contrast, they continued to be successful, and sportsmen were targeted because it was felt their teamwork experience made them good soldiers. This poster appeals to the masculine nature of Australian sporting culture, implying 'real sportsmen' volunteer for the 'real game'. It features vignettes of Australia's most popular sports, including cricket, rugby, Australian Rules football, boxing and racing.

Jacka VC also featured on other Australian recruiting posters, including a different version of *Enlist in the Sportsmen's 1000* published in 1917.

ON LES AURA! (WE'LL GET THEM!)

Abel Faivre (1876–1945)
Published in France, 1916

The French authorities used posters in much the same way as the British government, although conscription had been introduced in pre-war France, making the issue of recruiting posters redundant. Instead, official posters, like this famous design by Abel Faivre, concentrated on maintaining morale and raising money for the war effort.

The maintenance of morale became particularly important following the terrible French losses sustained during the Battle of Verdun in 1916. The title of this design, *On les aura!* ('We'll get them!'), is a quote from the French leader General Pétain, issued on 10 April 1916 during the battle itself. The remainder of the text implores Frenchmen to subscribe to the second National Defence Loan, a fund-raising scheme similar to those adopted in Britain, Germany and the United States. The figure of the gesturing determined-looking soldier was inspired by François Rude's sculpture of Liberty on the Arc de Triomphe in Paris, and shows the influence of national symbolism in wartime propaganda. With over 200,000 copies printed, *On les aura!* was probably the most famous French poster of the First World War.

GOD BLESS DADDY

B. E. Pike

Published in Australia, 1916

Australian men were not spared the 'recruiting guilt' technique used in the British Parliamentary Recruiting Committee's 1915 posters *Women of Britain say – "GO"*, and *Daddy, what did YOU do in the Great War?*

God Bless Daddy features a married woman, indicated by her wedding ring, kissing her young daughter in front of a portrait of an absent father in uniform. It is clearly intended to make single men feel guilty that they were 'shirking', or 'bludging' in the local vernacular, if they had not yet volunteered. Over 45,000 fathers with wives and children to look after had volunteered and put themselves in harm's way, despite their paternal responsibilities.

The emotional blackmail used in both the British and Australian 'guilt' posters was unpopular, and the negative connotations and association with guilt, anxiety, shame and embarrassment were not as successful recruiting techniques as posters that promoted duty and camaraderie. A second version of *God Bless Daddy*, created by the famous Australian artist Norman Lindsay and featuring the daughter kneeling in prayer before her seated mother, under the words 'God bless dear Daddy who is fighting the Hun and send him Help', was also produced in 1918.

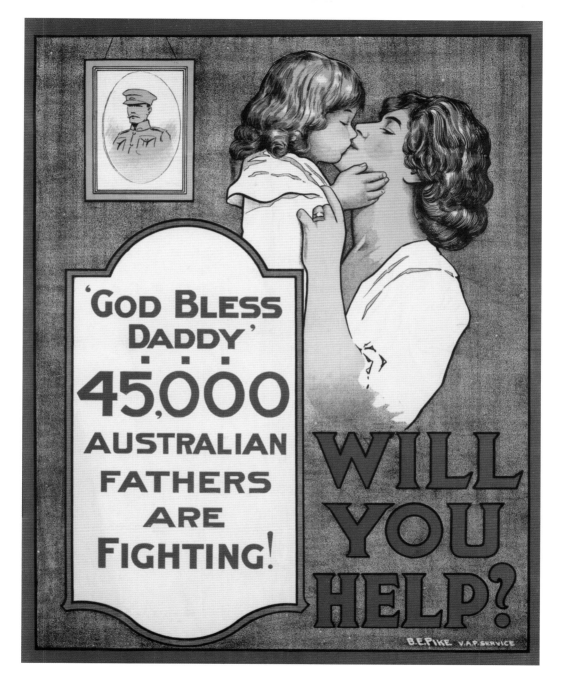

MUST IT COME TO THIS?

B. E. Pike

Published in Australia, 1916

Although the threat of actual invasion was very unlikely, the close proximity of German colonies in the Pacific to northern Australia had caused unease since the late nineteenth century. These colonies, including New Guinea, Samoa and the Solomon Islands, were actually the first German territories to be captured by the Entente powers during the war, when they fell to Australian and New Zealand expeditionary forces in August and September 1914.

With their seizure, the direct threat to Australia was extinguished, but Australian posters continued to play upon the paranoia this threat engendered for propaganda purposes long after it ceased to be real. This poster typifies that message. It features a caricature of Kaiser Wilhelm II, the shadow of his greedy right hand looming over Australia, as he reaches out across the globe from the direction of Europe.

The message is clear: although the war might have moved away from Australia's immediate vicinity and was being fought in far-off theatres, the Kaiser was still a threat to Australia. It was intended to make viewers consider what a German victory in Europe might mean back in Australia – would that direct threat of invasion become real again in the future?

A similarly themed poster entitled *Australians, Arise!* featured a map of Australia with the name 'Australia' struck through in red, and replaced by 'New Germany'. All the state capital cities were also crossed out and given German names.

NOW IT'S TIME TO JOIN THE ARMY

F. Boys

Published in India, 1916

While home service conscription was introduced for British residents of India, it did not apply to native Indians. All the native Indian troops who fought in the war did so voluntarily.

In 1914 the Indian Army was the largest all-volunteer army in the world, with over 240,000 regulars under arms. It was also one of the most experienced, dealing with almost constant skirmishes along the North-West Frontier and serving in other parts of the British Empire.

Although the Indian Army was impressive in size, it still needed expansion to meet the needs of its widespread deployments during the war, including Mesopotamia, Egypt, Palestine, East Africa, Europe and home service on the Frontier. Against the usual annual intake of fifteen thousand, by 1918 over 1.3 million men had volunteered as a result of the recruiting campaign.

This poster, printed in the state of Karnataka's Kannada language, reads: 'Now it's time to join the army. Get 8 acres of land and 75 rupees as prize money.' The smiling Indian havildar – the equivalent of sergeant – proudly holds up his medal. He is pointing to green fields in the background, reinforcing the offer of land in exchange for service.

In total over 1.7 million men served with the Indian Army in the First World War, suffering casualties of over 64,000 killed and a further 69,000 wounded.

ಇದೀಗ ಸಮಯ.

ನೀನು ಈಗ ಸೈನ್ಯಕ್ಕೆ ದಾಖಲಾದರೆ.

೮ ಎಕರೆಜಮೀನು ಮತ್ತು
75ರೂಪಾಯಿ ಬಹುಮಾನ ಸಿಕ್ಕುತ್ತೆ.

ಹೆಚ್ಚುತಪಶೀಲುಯೆಲ್ಲಾ ಡಿಸ್ಟ್ರಿಕ್ಟು ಮತ್ತುತಾಲ್ಲೂಕು ಕಛೇರಿಗಳ್ಲ್ಲಿ ದೊರಿಯುತ್ತೆ.

BUSHMEN & SAWMILL HANDS WANTED

Published in Canada, 1916

Just as natural athletes were sought for their existing teamwork and athleticism, those with labour skills in physically challenging jobs were in demand. This was particularly the case for specialist labourers who had experience in jobs needed for the war effort, such as miners and foresters.

In 1916 the British Government requested Canada to form a specialist forestry battalion for service in Britain and France, where foresters were in short supply. The forestry industry was one of Canada's most important and developed industries at the time.

With its headquarters in Ottawa, the 224th Forestry Battalion raised over 1,600 volunteers in just over six weeks. By the end of the war the foresters numbered over 35,000, and several battalions had been formed into the Canadian Forestry Corps (CFC). The CFC was tasked with skill-specific work, such as clearing woods for camps and airfields, using the lumber for construction materials, and cutting railway sleepers, trench supports and duckboards.

Other versions of this poster were also produced. One had the lumberjack in the same pose, next to a vignette of tree trunks being floated in a river. Another featured a lumberjack working a long saw into a recently felled tree, whilst a companion clears away previously felled trunks on a sledge in the background.

THE BOYS ARE DOING SPLENDIDLY

Published for the British West Indies Regiment, Kingston Jamaica, c. 1916

The British West Indies Regiment (BWIR) was raised in October 1915 from volunteers living in Jamaica, Trinidad and Tobago, Barbados, the Bahamas, British Honduras, Grenada, British Guiana, the Leeward Islands, St Lucia and St Vincent. The majority of the 15,600 eventual recruits came from Jamaica, and served with the British forces in north Africa, France, Mesopotamia and Palestine.

This poster was aimed at potential recruits in the Bahamas and was probably published in early 1916 after two initial 'contingents' of local men had already arrived in the listed war theatres. In total 486 Bahamians volunteered for the BWIR, with others serving in the regular British, Canadian and American armies.

Stylistically, the poster echoes those published in Britain during the opening weeks of the war, with the royal arms prominently displayed at the top and a clear injunction to fight for the King. Other recruiting posters published in the British West Indies were similarly unambiguous; reminding locals that it was their duty to defend the 'mother country', even though many would have had no direct ties with Great Britain.

B. W. I. R.

THE BOYS ARE DOING SPLENDIDLY
IN
EGYPT
MESOPOTAMIA
FRANCE

ANOTHER
BAHAMAS CONTINGENT
WILL BE SAILING SOON.

Roll up
Men

Make it
the Best

GOD SAVE THE KING!

The Gleaner Co., Ltd., Printers, 148, 150 & 152 Harbour Street, Kingston, Jamaica.

137

1917

FREE TRAINING FOR MUNITION WORKERS

Published by the London County Council, February 1917

Recruitment of men for war service left significant gaps in the workforce in Britain. The limited types and number of jobs available to women pre-war were expanded to meet labour shortages. Women filled non-traditional roles in agriculture, transport, hospitals and industry.

This London County Council poster appealing for women workers features the interior of a modern, clean munitions factory, with four lines of lathes for machining munitions and women staffing the entire factory. It makes clear that the training required to do this work is provided free.

The idea of an all-female staff running an important factory without a male foreman present would have been challenging to many people at the time, but women's traditional roles in the home and society were changing. In the years immediately preceding the war, the suffragette movement had vigorously campaigned for an improvement to women's rights, including the right to vote. They had also engaged in militant activities and hunger strikes to pursue their campaign, but upon the outbreak of war these were suspended in favour of supporting the war effort.

Women readily took up traditional male jobs, and their success in such roles forced many to reassess female capabilities. During the First World War, roughly two million women took up traditional male roles. After the war many were replaced by returning men, but the cause of women's rights had been advanced.

LONDON COUNTY COUNCIL.

CLASSES CONDUCTED AT THE REQUEST OF THE MINISTRY OF MUNITIONS

FREE TRAINING FOR MUNITION WORKERS

WOMEN URGENTLY WANTED TO TRAIN FOR FULL TIME EMPLOYMENT

· PARTICULARS AND APPLICATION FORMS FROM THE EDUCATION ·
· OFFICER, L.C.C. EDUCATION OFFICES, VICTORIA EMBANKMENT, W.C. ·

FEBRUARY, 1917   R.BLAIR, EDUCATION OFFICER

141

WOMEN CLERKS WANTED AT ONCE

Published by the Ministry of National Service, 1917

From August 1914 women's groups campaigned for their own uniformed services to support the war effort. The unrelenting casualty rate on the Western Front finally persuaded the British government to raise a Women's Army Auxiliary Corps (WAAC) in December 1916 to release experienced soldiers from non–combatant roles.

Recruitment was initially organised by the Ministry of National Service with women employed in a variety of roles, including secretaries, telephonists, cooks and waitresses. Although issued with a uniform and subject to the principles of military discipline, the WAAC had a different command structure from that of the regular army. Officers were called 'officials', while sergeants were referred to as 'forewomen' and the other ranks as 'workers', thereby suggesting a workplace structure rather than a military formation.

Most members of the WAAC were based in the United Kingdom, but about seven thousand served in France, where there was an urgent need for clerks in the support areas, as indicated by this poster. According to a contemporary recruiting pamphlet, the ideal candidate for an overseas posting would be aged twenty-five to thirty-five 'with a good education' and 'a little experience of clerical work'. To allay any fears of impropriety, potential recruits (and their parents) were informed that 'acceptable candidates' would be 'housed in hostels… under the careful supervision of capable women appointed by the War Office'.

NATIONAL N·S SERVICE
WOMEN CLERKS
WANTED AT ONCE

FOR
SERVICE IN FRANCE
WITH THE BRITISH ARMY

For Conditions of Service and Application Forms
APPLY
WOMEN'S SECTION NATIONAL SERVICE DEPARTMENT,
ST. ERMIN'S WESTMINSTER, S.W.I.

YES – COMPLETE VICTORY. IF YOU EAT LESS BREAD

Published by the Ministry of Food, 1917

As the war progressed, German naval blockades and unrestricted U-boat attacks on British merchant ships caused severe shortages of some foodstuffs and materials in the United Kingdom. Government posters, such as this one issued by the Ministry of Food in 1917, encouraged people to consume less and save more in an effort to conserve precious resources.

The loaf, a staple of the British diet, came to symbolise the campaign, with all sections of society asked to 'eat less bread' as a patriotic act that would help Britain win the war. The national Food Control Committee recommended a maximum weekly allowance of 4 pounds of bread per person, darkly suggesting that if this voluntary injunction were not adhered to then the government would be forced to introduce rationing. Not everyone approved of this level of state interference in their domestic lives, and posters alone proved inadequate in altering patterns of consumption. Prices soared for many basic food items, causing inequality of supply and public discontent. Rationing for bacon, ham, cheese, margarine, butter, milk and sugar was eventually introduced in 1918 to ensure a fairer system of distribution. Bread, however, was never actually in short supply in Britain, despite the poster slogans, and was kept off the ration to maintain morale.

WHICH PICTURE WOULD YOUR FATHER LIKE TO SHOW HIS FRIENDS?

Harry John Weston (1874–1938)

Published by the New South Wales Recruiting Committee, 1917

This poster in eye-catching yellow and black with a red diagonal band across it, features a dutiful soldier in the upper left, and a sportsman in the lower right relaxing with a drink on a deckchair surrounded by sports equipment.

It is an interesting combination of the often repeated appeal to sportsmen and the 'shirker' style of guilt posters. It suggests that fit and keen sportsmen should enlist (as with earlier sportsmen-themed posters) whilst at the same time suggesting such men were shaming their families, and especially their fathers, by not joining up.

This is part of a series of recruitment posters produced by the Australian 'Win the War League', a committee established in early 1917 by the Women's State Recruiting Committee in South Australia. On 27 April 1917 they held a 'Win the War Day', where the wives, daughters and sisters of troops serving abroad participated in a march through the streets of Adelaide, and sold badges to raise funds for the war effort. They promoted recruitment, and conducted fund-raising activities with the aim of bringing the war to a speedy and successful end.

The Tasmanian-born artist Harry Weston was a prominent producer of Australian wartime recruitment posters.

BRITISHERS ENLIST TO-DAY

Guy Lipscombe (1881–1952)

Published by the British government for distribution in the United States, 1917

The patriotic symbolism of the Union Flag was extensively used in the United Kingdom and overseas to rally support for the war against Germany. This poster was first published in Britain by the PRC in June 1915 with the alternative wording 'Its Our Flag. Fight for it. Work for it.' The version here was re-issued for the United States market in 1917 as part of a recruiting drive to encourage British citizens to return home and join the army.

In an associated article for the *Los Angeles Times* (9 September 1917), the officer in charge of British recruiting in Southern California sternly reminded compatriots living in America that it was their 'duty to at once enlist for service under the British flag', adding that in England 'boys of 19 are helping to fight your battles for you. You cannot remain in this country in sheltered safety while your fellows are waging this great struggle against a ruthless enemy.'

149

I WANT YOU FOR U.S. ARMY

James Montgomery Flagg (1877–1960)

Published by the United States government, April 1917

Inspired by the effectiveness of British recruiting posters, Montgomery Flagg designed his own version of Alfred Leete's Lord Kitchener poster (1914) for the American market, modelling the figure of Uncle Sam on an older version of himself. As with Leete's image, *I Want YOU for U.S. Army* first appeared on the pages of a magazine (*Leslie's Weekly*) before being translated to the hoardings as a government recruiting poster in 1917.

Recruitment in the United States remained voluntary throughout the war, with recruiting posters playing an important role in justifying the conflict and promoting a patriotic response. This image was immensely successful both in encapsulating American patriotism and aiding recruitment. Over 4 million copies were printed between 1917 and 1918, far outstripping any comparable design produced in Britain. The image resonated with the American public so well that it was revived for the Second World War. Its continuing popularity is still seen today through countless reinventions and parodies.

151

IT'S WORTH WHILE! THAT'S WHY

James Prinsep Beadle (1863–1947)

Published by the National War Savings Committee, 1917

War Savings Certificates were introduced by the British government in 1916 to help finance the war. At 15s 6d each, the certificates were more affordable than national War Bonds and could be redeemed for £1 (20 shillings) after five years. For those who could not afford to pay the full cost of the certificate immediately, the government offered the option of a War Savings Card that was completed through the purchase of 6d stamps and then exchanged for a certificate.

The associated publicity campaign targeted small investors with limited disposable income, represented in this poster by two working men discussing the merits of the scheme. Other posters stressed the patriotic responsibility of civilians to invest whatever they could in War Bonds and Savings Certificates, pointing out the dual benefit of helping to secure victory and achieving a good return on outlay.

War Savings Certificates proved to be extremely popular, raising £207 million by the end of the war. They were still being issued in 1919 and were re-launched as National Savings Certificates in 1920.

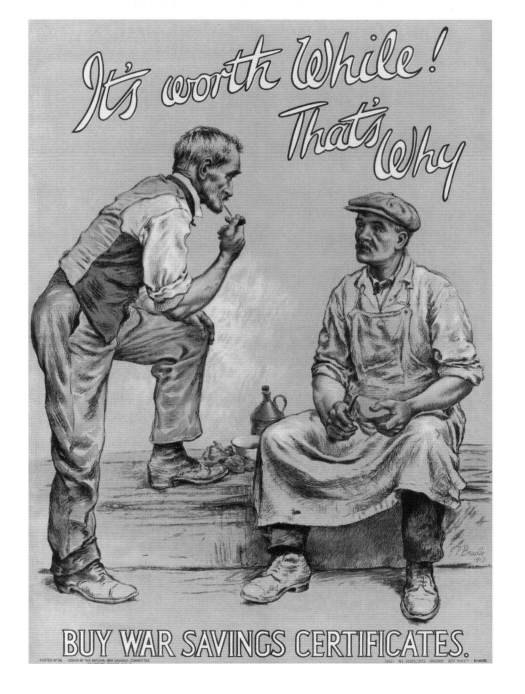

153

MUNITIONEERS' OPEN-AIR FETE

Dorothy Cottington-Taylor

Published on behalf of the Lady Superintendent's Benevolent Fund, Royal Arsenal, Woolwich, July 1917

The Lady Superintendent's Benevolent Fund was one of over ten thousand charities created during the First World War to provide financial assistance for those brought into personal hardship by the conflict, including refugees, wounded servicemen and the families of those killed in action. Charitable fund-raising raised £29 million in 1916 alone, while the largest charity, the Red Cross Society, raised over £22 million between 1914 and 1918.

The poster features a female munitions worker (or 'munitioneer') welcoming the viewer to a fund-raising event held in Shrewsbury Park, Plumstead, on 21 July 1917. Such events would have been a familiar part of the British scene during the summer months and helped create a shared unity of purpose in support of the war effort. To stress the internationalism of Britain's role, the Union Flag is displayed with equal status on a line of flags representing the Allied nations, including Japan, the United States (which had only recently entered the war in April 1917), France, Russia (with the colours in the wrong order) and Italy.

Several organisations providing welfare to ex-servicemen were amalgamated in 1921 to form the Royal British Legion. In November 1921 the British Legion launched its first annual poppy appeal, which continues to support former service personnel to this day.

ROYAL ARSENAL, WOOLWICH
MUNITIONEERS'
OPEN AIR FÊTE

IN AID OF THE LADY SUPERINTENDENT'S
(MISS L.C.BARKER)
BENEVOLENT FUND
TO BE HELD IN
SHREWSBURY
PARK
PLUMSTEAD
(By kind permission of the Trustees of the Crole-Wyndham Estate)
On Saturday 21st July 1917. at 5.p.m.
TICKETS 6d.

Obtainable at the Lady Superintendent's
Office, Manorway Gate; from the Welfare
Supervisor's; the Factories' Committees; the
Hostels and Canteens; the Pioneer Office,
New Street, Woolwich, S.E.18.

SEE SMALL HANDBILLS

Cottington Taylor

EVERY FIT WOMAN CAN RELEASE A FIT MAN

Published on behalf of the Women's Army Auxiliary Corps, 1917

The campaign to persuade young women to join the WAAC bore many similarities with the army recruiting drive of 1914–15. In this anonymous design, a line of smiling recruits wave cheerfully at the viewer beneath a prominent Union Flag to emphasise their patriotic endeavour. By October 1917 an estimated five thousand female volunteers were needed each week to release more soldiers for front-line service. The gesturing figure of a confident young woman in khaki (seen here) was extensively used in associated press advertisements and recruiting leaflets and became a symbol of the wider mobilisation of society in the final phase of the war.

Recruitment was organised through the local employment exchanges, which offered women a range of opportunities with the WAAC previously reserved for men, such as vehicle maintenance and engineering. More traditional needlework skills were much in demand by the Royal Flying Corps (part of the army in 1917), which required two thousand recruits a month to make and repair canvas aeroplane wings, while many more were needed as storekeepers and clerks. These jobs conferred higher status on female employees than pre-war domestic service or shop work and helped to change the perception of 'women's work' in the post-war era.

1918

FEED THE GUNS
WITH WAR BONDS

Bert Thomas (1883–1966)

Published by the National War Savings Committee, 1918

Together with War Loans and Savings Certificates, War Bonds enabled depositors to support the war effort and achieve a return on their investment. From 1917 posters played a very important part in selling the bonds and creating a visual unity for local fund-raising campaigns, such as 'Feed the Guns Weeks' and 'Tank Weeks'.

This design, by the well-known commercial artist Bert Thomas, is typical of several produced in the final year of the war. The depiction of a field gun and crew in graphic silhouette is intended to convey a powerful sense of forward momentum, which the purchase of War Bonds would help sustain. Other posters showed stylised images of tanks and aeroplanes in action, although the horrors of the battlefield were strenuously avoided.

In total, the National War Savings Committee (NWSC) published over two hundred poster designs on behalf of the British government – a huge achievement, eclipsing even the astonishing output of the Parliamentary Recruiting Committee earlier in the war.

Bert Thomas produced several of the most memorable designs and was given the status of official war artist working for the NWSC. His most famous wartime poster of a grinning, pipe-smoking cockney captioned 'Arf a 'Mo', Kaiser!' had first appeared as a private commission for the *Weekly Dispatch* in November 1914. After the war, Thomas continued his career as a successful artist and was a regular contributor to *Punch* magazine and *London Opinion*.

FEED THE GUNS WITH WAR BONDS AND HELP TO BRING THEM DOWN

Published by the National War Savings Committee, 1918

Another of the War Bonds posters asking investors to 'feed the guns', this issue is for anti-aircraft batteries rather than front-line artillery. The action is focused on the recognisable silhouette of the London skyline, dominated by St Paul's Cathedral, where searchlights and anti-aircraft batteries engage two German biplanes.

The strategic bombing of British cities by Germany is better remembered from the Second World War, but it happened in the First World War as well. Following the Zeppelin raids of 1915, defences were improved, and incendiary rounds were introduced to shoot down the highly flammable airships. This forced Germany to abandon Zeppelin raids in September 1916 and look for a long-range bomber aeroplane as an alternative.

The first German aeroplane raids on the capital, using Gotha bombers, began in 1917 and inflicted substantial civilian casualties. This poster, which eerily anticipates Second World War imagery, implies that the viewer can stop the attacks by buying War Bonds. The anti-aircraft batteries did have a positive impact, forcing the bombers to raid at night, which was less effective, and many Gothas were lost to navigation and landing errors in the dark. Regular raids ended in February 1918. A final vengeful raid was launched in May 1918, by which time over 80,000 kg of bombs had been dropped on England in a foretaste of what was to come in the next conflict.

162

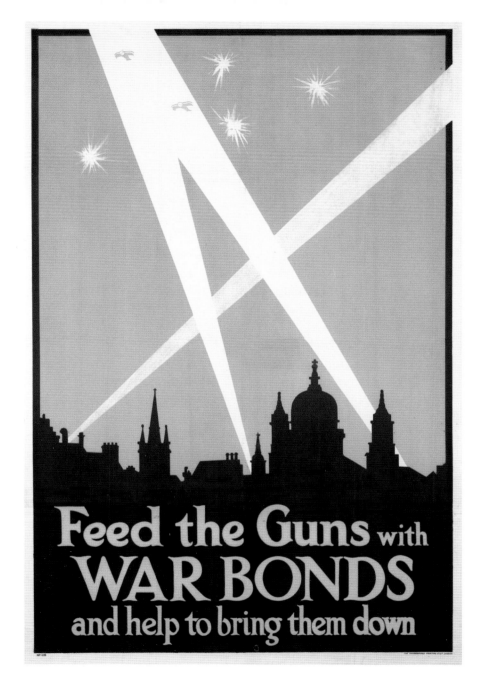

163

THE GIRL BEHIND THE MAN BEHIND THE GUN

Published on behalf of the Queen Mary's Army Auxiliary Corps, 1918

In April 1918 the WAAC was re-designated the Queen Mary's Army Auxiliary Corps (QMAAC) after its new patron and in recognition of the bravery of those members of the Corps serving overseas. The latter had been tested by the German advance of March 1918, when the WAAC had displayed courage and discipline during evacuation from the danger areas. On other occasions, too, members of the Corps based at depots in France and Flanders shared the dangers of their male colleagues. On 30 May 1918, for example, nine women were killed in an air raid at Abbeville.

   Despite the inherent dangers, recruiting posters for the QMAAC continued to use the visual language of pre-war girls' adventure stories and comics. Members of the Corps were typically portrayed as cheerful and rosy-cheeked in testimony to their healthy lifestyles. In this poster the gesturing figure from the 1917 recruiting campaign welcomes the potential recruit to a rural army base that has more than a passing resemblance to a Girl Guide camp of the period.

   During its brief existence, over 57,000 women enlisted with the WAAC/QMAAC. The unit was gradually wound down after the war and formally disbanded on 27 September 1921. A new version, the Auxiliary Territorial Service, was raised in December 1938 in response to the threatened war with Nazi Germany. Many former QMAACs rejoined, helping to create an *esprit de corps* in the tradition of the pioneering female soldiers of the First World War.

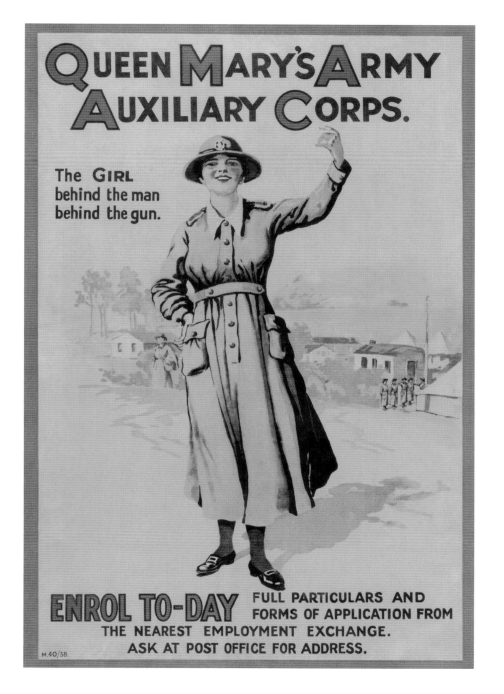

BACK HIM UP. BUY WAR BONDS

Frank Brangwyn (1867–1956)

Published by the National War Savings Committee, 1918

Frank Brangwyn's graphic poster for the 1918 autumn War Bonds campaign was unlike any other published in Britain during the war. For the first and only time, the conflict is represented as a brutal and desperate struggle between ordinary men. Gone is the cheery, cartoon-like depiction of British soldiery, replaced by a battle-hardened killer, while his German counterpart (typically depicted as the pitiless Hun) is drawn here with humanity and pathos. An even more violent version was published in vertical format with the alternative wording, 'Put strength in the final blow. Buy War Bonds'. In both cases, the act of buying War Bonds is directly linked with the action of the British soldier bayoneting his foe.

Such an unromantic depiction of war might have been expected to raise objections, but there is little evidence that either the government or the public found the image offensive. Brangwyn himself argued that no image could be too graphic to help bring the war to a close. However, the realistic portrayal did not represent a shift in government policy towards war poster imagery, as the design was speculatively submitted rather than directly commissioned by the National War Savings Committee.

Brangwyn, a well-established and respected artist, designed over eighty posters for the war effort, often waiving his usual fee. In addition to his work for the War Bonds and recruiting campaigns, Brangwyn produced a number of posters in support of civilian charities, especially for the relief of Belgium – the country of his birth and early childhood.

HONOUR AND GLORY

Published in France, 1918

This French poster refers to the arrival of the British 47th Division into Lille and features the blue, white and red stripes of the Tricolore flag.

The French city, close to the Belgian border, fell to the German Army very early in the war on 27 August 1914. It remained in their possession until almost the end of the conflict. But as the Allies' Hundred Days Offensive of 1918 wore on, the German occupation became untenable.

In September 1918, the German 6th Army evacuated Lille, destroying several bridges as they departed. Although British soldiers were first to arrive at the outskirts of the city, they waited to ensure the first troops to enter were French – giving them the honour of liberating their own city. Having played a key role in rebuffing the German Spring Offensive, the 47th (London) Division formally entered Lille on 28 October, where they were greeted as liberators by the citizens. It was the Division's final triumphant act of the war, which ended less than two weeks later.

Similar posters were printed by the civic authorities in towns and cities throughout the former Franco–Belgian war zone to welcome their liberators and celebrate the end of the conflict.

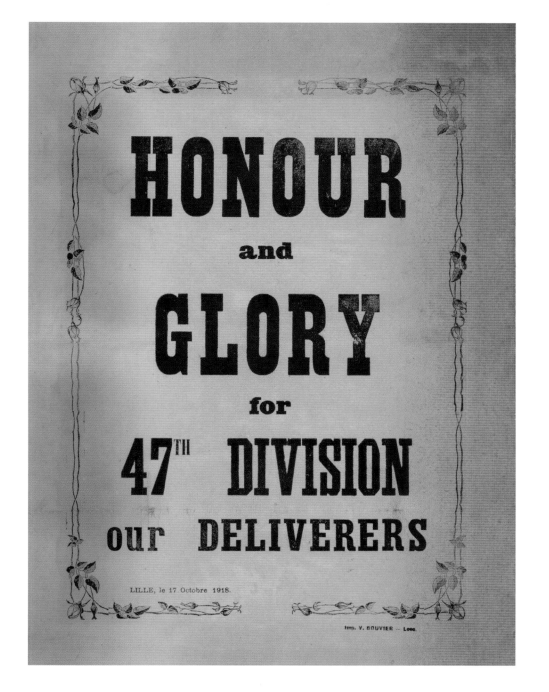

FURTHER READING

Aulich, Jim, and Hewitt, John. *Seduction or Instruction? First World War Posters in Britain and Europe*. Manchester University Press, 2007.

Aulich, James. *Weapons of Mass Communication*. Thames & Hudson in association with Imperial War Museum, London, 2007.

Hadley, Frederick, and Pegler, Martin. *Posters of the Great War*. Pen & Sword Books Limited, 2013.

Hardie, Martin, and Sabin, Arthur K. *War Posters Issued by Belligerent and Neutral Nations 1914–19*. London, 1920.

Hiley, Nicholas. 'Sir Hedley Le Bas and the Origins of Domestic Propaganda in Britain 1914–17', *European Journal of Marketing*, volume 21 issue 8, 1987.

Hiley, Nicholas. ' *"Kitchener Wants You"* and *"Daddy, What Did You Do in the Great War?"* – the Myth of British Recruiting Posters'. *Imperial War Museum Review*, 11, 1997.

James, Pearl (editor). *Picture This: World War I Posters and Visual Culture (Studies in War, Society and the Military)*. University of Nebraska Press, 2010.

Ormiston, Rosalind. *First World War Posters*. Flame Tree Publishing, 2013.

Rickards, Maurice. *Posters of the First World War.* London, 1969.

Sheldon, Cyril. *A History of Poster Advertising*. London, 1937.

Simkins, Peter. *Kitchener's Army – The Raising of the New Armies 1914–16*. Manchester University Press, 1988.

Taylor, James. *Your Country Needs You: The Secret History of the Propaganda Poster*. Saraband Limited, 2013.

Thatcher, Martyn, and Quinn, Anthony. *The Amazing Story of the Kitchener Poster*. Funfly Design, 2013.

INDEX